D0473790

Server Load Balancing

Server Load Balancing

Tony Bourke

O'REILLY®

Beijing · Cambridge · Farnham · Köln · Paris · Sebastopol · Taipei · Tokyo

Server Load Balancing
by Tony Bourke

Copyright © 2001 O'Reilly & Associates, Inc. All rights reserved.
Printed in the United States of America.

Published by O'Reilly & Associates, Inc., 101 Morris Street, Sebastopol, CA 95472.

Editor: Jim Sumser

Production Editor: Matt Hutchinson

Cover Designer: Emma Colby

Printing History:

August 2001:   First Edition.

Nutshell Handbook, the Nutshell Handbook logo, and the O'Reilly logo are registered trademarks of O'Reilly & Associates, Inc. Alteon WebOS, Foundry ServerIron, Cisco WebNS, Cisco CSS, F5 Network's BIG-IP, and Arrowpoint are registered trademarks. Many of the designations used by manufacturers and sellers to distinguish their products are claimed as trademarks. Where those designations appear in this book, and O'Reilly & Associates, Inc. was aware of a trademark claim, the designations have been printed in caps or initial caps. The association between the image of a jacana and the topic of server load balancing is a trademark of O'Reilly & Associates, Inc.

While every precaution has been taken in the preparation of this book, the publisher assumes no responsibility for errors or omissions, or for damages resulting from the use of the information contained herein.

ISBN: 0-596-00050-2
[M]

Table of Contents

Preface

This book is meant to be a resource for anyone involved in the design, production, overseeing, or troubleshooting of a site that employs server load balancing (SLB). Managers and other high-level people can use this book to improve their understanding of the overall technology. Engineers and site architects can use this book to give insight into their designs and implementations of SLB. Technicians can use this book to help configure and troubleshoot SLB implementations, as well as other in-the-trenches work.

This book came about because of the almost nonexistent resources for SLB that exist today. Most of the information and resources for an SLB implementation come from the vendor of the particular product that you use or are looking to use. Through my own trials and tribulations, I realized that there was a need for a third-party resource—one that was unbiased and had the users' interests at heart. While most or all of the vendors have good intentions in reference to what they tell you, they can still be clouded by the bottom line of their own sales figures.

Because SLB is relatively new, there is a lack of standardized terminology for concepts associated with the technology. Because of this lack of standardization, this book adopts a particular vocabulary that, though similar, does not match the vocabulary you may have adopted with a particular vendor. This was deliberately done to provide an even, unbiased basis for the discussion of SLB and its terminology.

This book includes a section devoted to configuring four of the SLB vendors. Those vendors are (in alphabetical order) Alteon WebSystems (*http://www.alteonwebsystems.com*); Cisco Systems, Inc., which includes their CSS-11000 (formerly known as Arrowpoint) line of products (*http://www.cisco.com*); F5 Networks, Inc., makers of BIG-IP (*http://www.f5.com*); and Foundry Networks, Inc. (*http://www.foundrynetworks.com*). These are not the only vendors in the SLB industry; this book would be well over a thousand pages if it were to cover all the vendors. These vendors represent the market leaders and the more popular among the lot. Though one section of this book is dedicated to these vendors, the other two can still provide a valuable resource no matter which SLB vendor you choose.

There is more than one way to skin a cat, as the old adage goes, and that is particularly true of the networking world. The methods shown in this book are tried-and-true implementations that I have worked with and have helped to develop over the few years SLB has been around. My ways aren't the only ways, nor are they necessarily the best ways, but they've served me well, and I hope they serve you, too.

This book assumes that the reader is relatively familiar with the basic, day-to-day workings of the IP suite of protocols, Ethernet (regular, Fast, or Gigabit), and the Internet in general. There are many great books that delve into the magic and inner workings of these subjects, if the need should arise. However, to understand load balancing, it is not necessary to know the byte length of an Ethernet frame header.

Overview

This book is divided into three parts. Part I concentrates on the theories and concepts of Server Load Balancing. Part II concentrates on the implementation and network topology of load balancers. Part III is a configuration guide to four significant load-balancing products on the market.

Part I: Concepts and Theories of Server Load Balancing

Chapter 1, *Introduction to Server Load Balancing*, glosses over the world of Server Load Balancing as a whole.

Chapter 2, *Concepts of Server Load Balancing*, delves into the concepts and terminology associated with Server Load Balancing. Since every vendor has its own jargon for essentially the same concepts, it's important to have a basic vocabulary for comparing one product and its features to another.

Chapter 3, *Anatomy of a Server Load Balancer*, goes into the networking process of Server Load Balancing. This chapter reviews the life of a packet as it travels from the user to the load balancer, from the load balancer to the server, from the server to the load balancer, and from the load balancer back to the user.

Chapter 4, *Performance Metrics*, discusses the various metrics associated with load-balancing performance.

Part II: Practice and Implementation
of Server Load Balancing

Chapter 5, *Introduction to Architecture*, goes into the actual guts of load-balancing devices and reviews the different paths that companies have taken in designing load-balancer hardware.

Chapter 6, *Flat-Based SLB Network Architecture*, delves into the flat-based network architecture, where the VIPs and real servers are on the same subnet. Flat-based is the most simple way of implementing a load-balanced network.

Chapter 7, *NAT-Based SLB Network Architecture*, deals with NAT-based SLB implementations, where the VIPs and real servers are on separate subnets. NAT-based SLB is more complicated, but can offer some advantages over the flat-based network, depending on your site's requirements.

Part III: Configuring Server Load Balancers

Chapter 8, *Alteon WebSystems*, presents two separate guides to configuring an Alteon load balancer for both scenarios laid out in Chapters 6 and 7.

Chapter 9, *Cisco's CSS (Formerly ArrowPoint) Configuration Guide*, presents two separate guides to configuring Cisco's CSS switches for both scenarios laid out in Chapters 6 and 7.

Chapter 10, *F5's BIG-IP*, presents two separate guides to configuring an F5 BIG-IP for both scenarios laid out in Chapters 6 and 7.

Chapter 11, *Foundry ServerIron Series*, presents two separate guides to configuring a Foundry ServerIron for both scenarios laid out in Chapters 6 and 7.

Appendix A, *Quick Command Guide*, is a quick reference to commonly performed administration tasks involving the load balancers featured in this book.

Appendix B, *Direct Server Return Configuration*, provides configuration examples for the setup of Direct Server Return (DSR).

Appendix C, *Sample Configurations*, is a quick reference to a multitude of possible load-balancing configurations and implementations. The illustrations in Appendix C are vendor-neutral.

This book was written using Microsoft Word and Visio. It was written during 2000–01 in New York City, usually in the wee hours of the night, and usually fueled by vegan chocolate chips and soy burgers.

Resources

Again, there is a multitude of resources available to people who are implementing or are planning to implement load balancers. Trade publications such as *Network World* (for which I have written and with which I have had a great experience) and *InfoWorld* do pieces on load balancing and the industry. The vendors are good resources to go to, but of course, they will be a little biased towards their products.

I run a mailing list for the discussion of load balancing, which can be found at *http://vegan.net/lb*. There are other resources linked to that site, including *http://vegan.net/MRTG*, which shows how to configure the freeware graphing program MRTG for use with load balancers and their metrics. MRTG, which can be found at *http://ee-staff.ethz.ch/~oetiker/webtools/mrtg/mrtg.html* is an absolutely marvelous tool written by Tobias Oetiker and Dave Rand. Never underestimate the power of pretty pictures.

Conventions Used in This Book

Throughout this book, I have used the following typographic conventions:

Constant width

> Used to indicate a language construct such as a language statement, a constant, or an expression. Lines of code also appear in constant width

Constant width bold

> Used to indicate user input

Italic

> Used to indicate commands, file extensions, filenames, directory or folder names, and functions

Constant width italic

> Used to indicate variables in examples

 This icon designates a note, which is an important aside to the nearby text.

 This icon designates a warning relating to the nearby text.

How to Contact Us

Please address comments and questions concerning this book to the publisher:

O'Reilly & Associates, Inc.
101 Morris St.
Sebastopol, CA 95472
(800) 998-9938 (in the U.S. or Canada)
(707) 829-0515 (international/local)
(707) 829-0104 (fax)

We have a web page for this book, where we list errata or any additional information. You can access this page at:

http://www.oreilly.com/catalog/serverload

To ask technical questions or comment on the book, send email to:

bookquestions@oreilly.com

For more information about our books, conferences, software, Resource Centers, and the O'Reilly Network, see our web site at:

http://www.oreilly.com

Acknowledgments

First off, I'd like to thank the vendors for their help. Their support teams have helped me when I needed clarification on a concept or a feature, as well as helping to ensure that their products were accurately represented.

At Cisco, I'd like to thank Dion Heraghty, Jim Davies, Kate Pence, and Jason La Carrubba from the ArrowPoint group; at F5, Rob Gilde, Ron Kim, and Dan Matte; at Alteon, Jimmy Wong, the incorrigible David Callisch, John Taylor, Andrew Hejnar, and Lori Hopkins; at Foundry, Chandra Kopparapu, Srini Ramadurai, and Jerry Folta. I'd also like to thank Mark Hoover for giving me additional insight into the industry.

Of course, I'd also like to thank my parents, Steve and Mary, for ensuring that I learned how to read and write (who knew that would pay off?); my sister Kristen, who kept bugging me to hurry up and finish the book; my former boss, Chris Coluzzi, the best boss I've ever had, who initially helped and encouraged me to write a book; and my coworkers at SiteSmith, Inc., my current employer, namely Treb Ryan, for supporting me in my speaking and writing endeavors.

I'd also like to thank my editor, Jim Sumser, who helped me through my first book, as well as my technical reviewer, Andy Neely, who made sure this book was on the level. And of course, my publisher, O'Reilly, the industry leader for many reasons—the way they handle their authors is definitely one of them.

I

Concepts and Theories of Server Load Balancing

1

Introduction to Server Load Balancing

While Server Load Balancing (SLB) could mean many things, for the purpose of this book it is defined as a process and technology that distributes site traffic among several servers using a network-based device. This device intercepts traffic destined for a site and redirects that traffic to various servers. The load-balancing process is completely transparent to the end user. There are often dozens or even hundreds of servers operating behind a single URL. In Figure 1-1, we see the simplest representation of SLB.

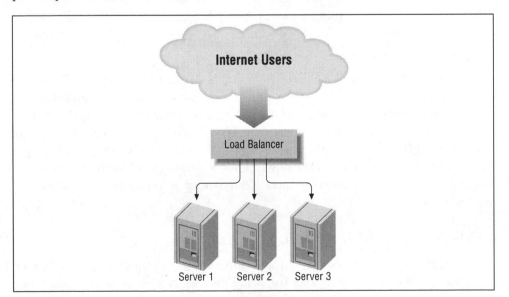

Figure 1-1. SLB simplified

A load balancer performs the following functions:

- Intercepts network-based traffic (such as web traffic) destined for a site.

- Splits the traffic into individual requests and decides which servers receive individual requests.

- Maintains a watch on the available servers, ensuring that they are responding to traffic. If they are not, they are taken out of rotation.

- Provides redundancy by employing more than one unit in a fail-over scenario.

- Offers content-aware distribution, by doing things such as reading URLs, intercepting cookies, and XML parsing.

In the Beginning

In its infancy, the Internet was mostly the playground of academia with very little general consumer use. Even when the Internet first started catching on around 1995 and personal use ballooned, web sites still weren't used much for commerce and, thus, were not "mission critical." A single server could easily handle the processing requirements of even one of the most popular sites of the day and, since there wasn't much commerce going on, it wasn't too big of a deal if the site went down. But as more and more businesses recognized the power and potential the Internet could offer, that started to change. People came up with clever ways to handle redundancy and scaling issues as they arose.

Bigger and Faster

When faced with a server pushed to its limits, one of the first instincts of a system administrator is to somehow beef it up. Adding more RAM, upgrading the processor, or adding more processors were all typical options. However, those measures could only scale so far. At some point, you'll max out the scalability of either a hardware platform or the operating system on which it runs. Also, beefing up a server requires taking the server down, and downtime is a concern that server upgrades don't address. Even the most redundant of server systems is still vulnerable to outages.

DNS-Based Load Balancing

Before SLB was a technology or a viable product, site administrators would (and sometimes still do) employ a load-balancing process known as DNS round robin. DNS round robin uses a function of DNS that allows more than one IP address to associate with a hostname. Every DNS entry has what is known as an A record, which maps a hostname (such as *www.vegan.net*) to an IP address (such as

208.185.43.202). Usually only one IP address is given for a hostname. Under ISC's DNS server, BIND 8, this is what the DNS entry for *www.vegan.net* would look like:

```
www.vegan.net.                    IN      A       208.185.43.202
```

With DNS round robin, it is possible to give multiple IP addresses to a hostname, distributing traffic more or less evenly to the listed IP addresses. For instance, let's say you had three web servers with IP addresses of 208.185.43.202, 208.185.43.203, and 208.185.43.204 that we wanted to share the load for the site *www.vegan.net*. The configuration in the DNS server for the three IP addresses would look like this:

```
www.vegan.net.                    IN      A       208.185.43.202
                                  IN      A       208.185.43.203
                                  IN      A       208.185.43.204
```

You can check the effect using a DNS utility known as *nslookup*, which would show the following for *www.vegan.net*:

```
[zorak]# nslookup www.vegan.net
Server:  ns1.vegan.net
Address:  198.143.25.15

Name:    www.vegan.net
Addresses:  208.185.43.202, 208.185.43.203, 208.185.43.204

>
```

The end result is that the traffic destined for *www.vegan.net* is distributed between the three IP addresses listed, as shown in Figure 1-2.

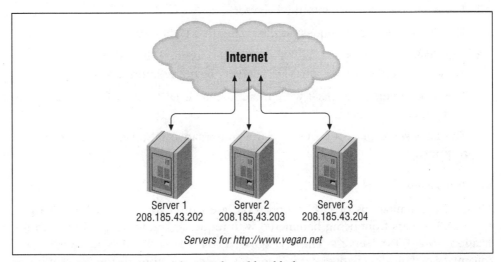

Figure 1-2. Traffic distribution by DNS-based load balancing

This seems like a pretty simple way to distribute traffic among servers, so why bother spending the money and time implementing SLB at all? The reason is that DNS round robin has several limitations, including unpredictable load distribution, caching issues, and a lack of fault-tolerance measures. An understanding of how DNS works will help to explain the problems of DNS-based load balancing.

DNS 101

DNS associates IP addresses with hostnames so that we don't have to memorize numbers; instead, we memorize domain names. A computer needs to know the IP address, however. To perform that translation, every computer connected to the Internet, whether it be a server or a dialup user's home machine, has one or more DNS servers configured. When a user types the URL of a hostname into his browser, for instance, the operating system sends a query to the configured DNS server requesting the IP address of that hostname. The DNS server doesn't usually have that information (unless it is cached, which is something we'll discuss later), so the domain name server looks up the domain name with one of the root servers. The root servers do not have the IP address information either, but they know who does, and report that to the user's DNS server. (Servers with the appropriate DNS information are known as the authoritative DNS servers. There are usually at least two listed for a domain, and you can find out what they are by using the *whois* utility supplied by most Unix distributions, or through several domain-registration web sites.) The query goes out to the authoritative name server, the IP address is reported back, and in a matter of seconds the web site appears on the user's screen. The entire process works like this:

1. The user types the URL into the browser.

2. The OS makes a DNS request to the configured DNS server.

3. The DNS server sees if it has that IP address cached. If not, it makes a query to the root servers to see what DNS servers have the information.

4. The root servers reply back with an authoritative DNS server for the requested hostname.

5. The DNS server makes a query to the authoritative DNS server and receives a response.

Caching issues

Many of the limitations of DNS round robin are caused by DNS caching. To prevent DNS servers from being hammered with requests, and to keep bandwidth utilization low, DNS servers employ quite a bit of DNS caching. Since DNS information typically changes very little, this is fine for normal functions. When a DNS server goes out and gets a DNS entry, it caches that entry until the entry expires, which can take anywhere from a few days to a week (that parameter is configurable). You can configure a domain to never cache, although some DNS servers throughout the world may ignore this and cache anyway.

Traffic distribution

Traffic distribution is one of the problems with DNS round robin that caching causes. DNS round robin is supposed to distribute traffic evenly among the IP addresses it has listed for a given hostname. If there are three IP addresses listed, then one-third of the traffic should go to each server. If four IP addresses are listed, then one-fourth of the traffic should go to each server. Unfortunately, this is not how round robin works in live environments. The actual traffic distribution can vary significantly. This is because individual users do not make requests to the authoritative name servers; they make requests to the name servers configured in their operating systems. Those DNS servers then make the requests to the authoritative DNS servers and cache the received information. Figure 1-3 shows a typical failure scenario with DNS-based load balancing.

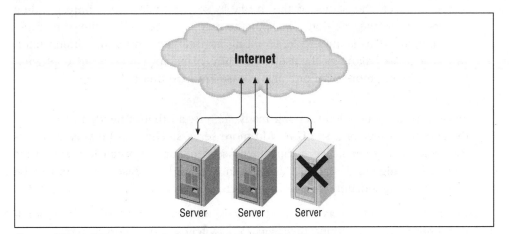

Figure 1-3. A failure scenario with DNS-based load balancing

The lack of DNS update speed is also an issue when demand increases suddenly, and more servers are required quickly. Any new server entries in DNS take a while to propagate, which makes scaling a site's capacity quickly difficult.

Evolution

It's now clear that better solutions to managing the problems of redundancy, scalability, and management were needed. Web sites were becoming more and more critical to business' existences. These days, downtime has a direct dollar value associated with it. Some sites lose thousands of dollars or more in revenue for every minute their sites are unavailable. SLB evolved from this need. A load balancer works by taking traffic directed at a site. One URL, one IP address, and the load balancer distribute the load. They balance the load by manipulating the network packets bound for the site and usually do it again on the way out. We'll discuss this in more detail in later chapters.

SLB has several benefits, which is why it is such a highly successful and widely employed technology. Three main benefits directly address the concerns and needs of highly trafficked, mission-critical web sites:

Flexibility

SLB allows the addition and removal of servers to a site at any time, and the effect is immediate. Among other advantages, this allows for the maintenance of any machine, even during peak hours with little or no impact to the site. A load balancer can also intelligently direct traffic using cookies, URL parsing, static and dynamic algorithms, and much more.

High availability

SLB can check the status of the available servers, take any nonresponding servers out of the rotation, and put them in rotation when they are functioning again. This is automatic, requiring no intervention by an administrator. Also, the load balancers themselves usually come in a redundant configuration, employing more than one unit in case any one unit fails.

Scalability

Since SLB distributes load among many servers, all that is needed to increase the serving power of a site is to add more servers. This can be very economical, since many small- to medium-sized servers can be much less expensive than a few high-end servers. Also, when site load increases, servers can be brought up immediately to handle the increase in traffic.

Load balancers started out as PC-based devices, and many still are, but now load-balancing functions have found their way into switches and routers as well.

Other Technologies

Other technologies have evolved to handle the scalability and management issues that modern Internet sites face. As stated, SLB works by intercepting and manipulating network packets destined for the servers. There are other technologies that address the same issues as SLB, but in different ways. There are also technologies that address issues that SLB does not address, but in similar ways, and sometimes with the same equipment.

Firewall Load Balancing

Firewall Load Balancing (FWLB) has been developed to overcome some of the limitations of firewall technologies. Most firewalls are CPU-based, such as a SPARC machine or an x86-based machine. Because of the processor limitations involved, the amount of throughput a firewall can handle is often limited. Processor speed, packet size, configuration, and several other metrics are all determining factors for what a firewall can do, but generally, they tend to max out at around 70 to 80 Mbps (Megabits per second) of throughput. Like SLB, FWLB allows for the implementation of several firewalls sharing the load in a manner similar to SLB. Because of the nature of the traffic, however, the configuration and technology are different. Figure 1-4 shows a common FWLB configuration.

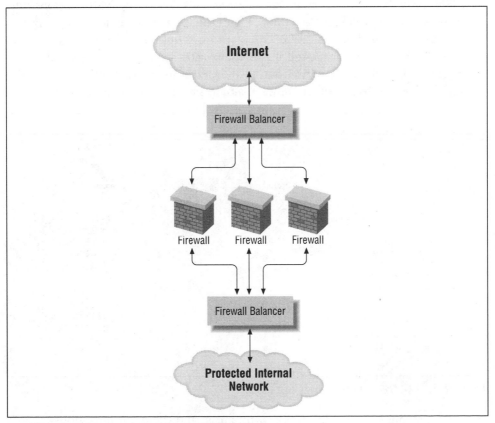

Figure 1-4. A common FWLB configuration

Global Server Load Balancing

Global Server Load Balancing (GSLB) has the same basic concept as SLB, but it distributes load to various locations as opposed to one location. SLB works on the

Local Area Network (LAN), while GSLB works on the Wide Area Network (WAN). There are several ways to implement GSLB, such as DNS-based and BGP-based (Border Gateway Protocol). There are two main reasons to implement GSLB, and to illustrate them we'll use an example of GLSB in action. Let's take the example of a site that has a presence in two different data centers, one in San Jose, California, and one in New York City (see Figure 1-5):

1. GSLB brings content closer to the users. With cross-country latency at around 60 ms (milliseconds) or more, it makes sense to bring the users as close to the servers as possible. For instance, it would make sense to send a user in North Carolina to a server in New York City, rather than to a server in San Jose, California.

2. GSLB provides redundancy in case any site fails. There are many reasons why an entire data-center installation can go offline, such as a fiber cut, a power outage, an equipment failure, or a meteor from outer space (as every summer New York City gets destroyed in some climactic scene in a Hollywood block-buster). Sites choosing not to put all their eggs in one basket can use GSLB technology to divert traffic to any remaining sites in case of site failures.

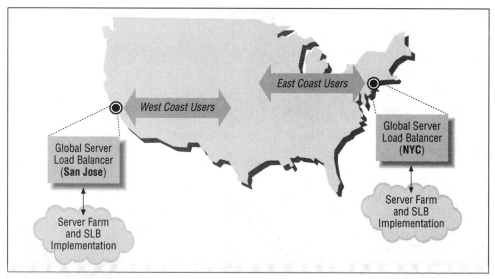

Figure 1-5. A GSLB example

GSLB as a technology is still a work in progress, and there are limitations to both the DNS and BGP-based methods. With DNS-based GSLB the way it is, there is no guarantee that all of the West Coast users will be directed to the West Coast, or all of the East Coast users will be directed to the East Coast, and that everyone will be directed to another site in the event of a site-wide failure. There are also state and persistence issues with the various fail-over methods. Vendors are currently working on solutions. Though not 100 percent effective, GSLB is still an important technolgy and is employed by many large-scale sites.

Clustering

Clustering offers a solution to the same problems that SLB addresses, namely high availability and scalability, but clustering goes about it differently. Clustering is a highly involved software protocol (proprietary to each vendor) running on several servers that concentrate on taking and sharing the load (see Figure 1-6). Rather than sitting in front of several servers and manipulating network packets like a network device, clustering involves a group of servers that accept traffic and divide tasks amongst themselves. This involves a fairly tight integration of server software. This is often called load balancing, and while the nomenclature is technically correct, I prefer clustering since it is application-based, reserving load balancing for the network-based aspect of the technology.

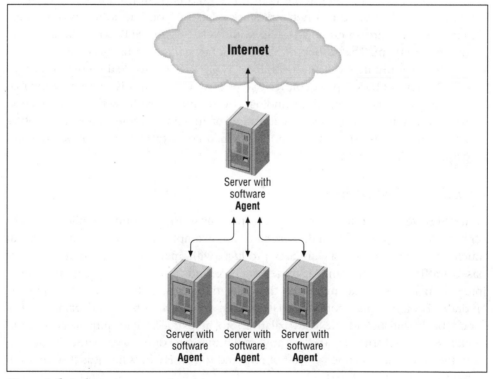

Figure 1-6. A clustering scenario

With clustering, there is a fairly tight integration between the servers in the cluster, with software deciding which servers handle which tasks and algorithms determining the work load and which server does which task, etc. Much like the Borg, a cluster acts as a single mind with a single purpose, and is very tightly integrated. SLB is different in that there is usually no interaction between the servers in any way, with the centralized mind being concentrated with the load balancers. There are several vendors offering clustering solutions, and some even play in the same market space in which SLB vendors operate. The vendors can vary greatly in how they handle clustering, but the scenario described is typical for clustering implementation.

SLB Versus Clustering

While there are advantages to having servers work together, there are several disadvantages to clustering. Since there is tight integration between the servers, special software is required and, as a result, a vendor will most likely support a limited number of platforms, such as Solaris or Windows 2000. Some vendors support only one platform. Also, a limited number of protocols are supported with this scheme—rarely anything more than HTTP. SLB is platform and OS neutral, so it works as long as there is a network stack. Heck, if you had a group of toasters running some weird operating system with web servers, SLB could balance the load between them. That is one of SLB's great tactical strengths. SLB will also support just about any network protocol, from HTTP to NFS, to Real Media, to almost any TCP- or UDP-based protocol, no matter how weird. SLB is extremely flexible in this regard. It is a simpler technology by design as well: with no interaction between the servers and a clear delineation of functions, there is less to troubleshoot, in most cases. An SLB design (if designed correctly) can be very simple and elegant, as well as powerful and functional.

Crossover Technology

Some SLB vendors offer features that are similar to clustering, while still subscribing to the church of SLB. Resonate, for example, is a product that runs in much the same fashion as an SLB product, with machines accepting network-based traffic and distributing it to servers. Like clustering, however, there is tight integration between the machines that take the network traffic and the servers. HydraWEB offers agent software that can run on the servers it load balances and report back statistics to the load balancers to help make determinations on individual server performance and on how much traffic to direct to a particular server. This agent software technology is not required to run HydraWEB; it is just an additional feature that is offered.

This is a book about SLB and SLB only, and while the other technologies are worthy of study, this is the extent of their coverage. The other technologies are as involved as SLB, and each deserves its own book. They are covered simply to delineate the technologies and give a reference to readers about how SLB fits into the grand scheme of Internet technologies.

2

Concepts of Server Load Balancing

The world of Server Load Balancing (and network-based load balancing in general) is filled with confusing jargon and inconsistent terminology. Because of the relative youth and the fierce competition of the SLB industry, vendors have come up with their own sets of terminology, which makes it difficult to compare one product and technology to another. Despite the confusing terms, however, the basic concepts remain the same.

This chapter breaks down the basic components associated with SLB and provides consistent terminology and definitions. With this guide in hand, it should be much easier to compare products and technologies and gain a better understanding of SLB as a whole by boiling SLB down to it's simplest elements.

Networking Basics

Server Load Balancing works its magic in the networking realm. While this book assumes that the reader has experience in networking, it may be beneficial to cover some common networking terms and concepts and their relation to SLB. O'Reilly's *Managing IP Networks with Cisco Routers* by Scott M. Ballew provides a good general review of basic networking concepts and strategies.

OSI Layer Model

When referring to load balancers, OSI layers are often mentioned. OSI was developed as a framework for developing protocols and applications that could interact seamlessly. It closely resembles the Internet IP world in which load balancers exist today.

The OSI model is broken into seven layers and is appropriately referred to as the 7-Layer Model. Each layer represents a separate abstraction layer and interacts only with its adjoining layers:

Layer 1

This is the lowest layer, often referred to as the "Physical" layer. The basic units of data, 1s and 0s, are transmitted on this layer electronically, such as with amplitude modulation on an Ethernet line or a Radio Frequency (RF) signal on a coaxial connection.

Layer 2

This layer refers to the method of organizing and encapsulating binary information for transport over a Layer 1 medium. Since SLB devices are almost always exclusively Ethernet-based, Layer 2 refers to Ethernet frames. An Ethernet frame consists of a header, a checksum (for error-correction), and a payload. Ethernet frames range in size, usually with a limit (known as Maximum Transmittable Units, or MTUs) of 1.5 KB for Ethernet, Fast Ethernet, and Gigabit Ethernet. Some devices support Jumbo Frames for Gigabit Ethernet, which is over 9,000 bytes.

Layer 3

Layer 3 devices are routers, which represent the level of information moved from one location to another in an intelligent manner (hence the clever name, router). IPv4 is the current standard for which Layer 3 IP packets are structured. An IP packet has a source IP address and a destination IP address in the header.

Layer 4

This layer deals with an IP address and a port. TCP and UDP are two protocols that run on this layer. They have a source and destination IP address in the header, as well as a source and destination port. The payload is an encapsulated IP packet.

Layers 5–7

Layers 5–7 involve URL load balancing and parsing. The URL may be complete (such as *http://www.vegan.net/home*) or may be a cookie embedded into a user session. An example of URL load balancing is directing traffic to *http://www.vegan.net/cgi-bin* through one group of servers, while sending *http://www.vegan.net/images* to another group. Also, URL load balancing can set persistence (discussed later in this chapter) based on the "cookie" negotiated between the client and the server.

The relation of the OSI layers to Server Load Balancing is outlined in Table 2-1.

Table 2-1. OSI layers and SLB

OSI layer	Function	Units	Example	Relation to SLB
Layer 1	Physical	1s and 0s	Cat 5 cable, SX fiber	This is the cabling used to plug into Layer 2 switches and hubs.
Layer 2	Data link	Ethernet frames	Ethernet switches, hubs	These devices are Ethernet switches or hubs; these aggregate traffic.
Layer 3	Network	IP addresses	Routers	These devices are routers, although SLB devices have router characteristics.
Layer 4	Transport	TCP, UDP, ICMP	TCP port 80 for HTTP, UDP port 161 for SNMP	This is the level typically referred to when discussing SLB. An SLB instance will involve an IP address and a TCP/UDP port.
Layers 5–7	Session, presentation, and application	URL, cookie	*http://www. vegan.net/home* or cookies	This refers to nything specifically looking into the packet or the URL, such as cookie information, specific URL, etc.

Server Load Balancers

A load balancer is a device that distributes load among several machines. As discussed earlier, it has the effect of making several machines appear as one. There are several components of SLB devices, which are discussed in detail.

VIPs

Virtual IP (VIP) is the load-balancing instance where the world points its browsers to get to a site. A VIP has an IP address, which must be publicly available to be useable. Usually a TCP or UDP port number is associated with the VIP, such as TCP port 80 for web traffic. A VIP will have at least one real server assigned to it, to which it will dispense traffic. Usually there are multiple real servers, and the VIP will spread traffic among them using metrics and methods, as described in the "Active-Active Scenario" section.

Servers

A server is a device running a service that shares the load among other services. A server typically refers to an HTTP server, although other or even multiple services would also be relevant. A server has an IP address and usually a TCP/UDP port associated with it and does not have to be publicly addressable (depending on the network topology).

Groups

While the term "group" is often used by vendors to indicate several different concepts, we will refer to it loosely as a group of servers being load balanced. The term "farm" or "server farm" would also be applicable to this concept.

User-Access Levels

A user-access level refers to the amount of control a particular user has when logged into a load balancer. Not only do different vendors refer to their access levels differently, but most employ very different access-level methods. The most popular is the Cisco style of user and enable (superuser) accounts. Another popular method is the Unix method of user-level access.

Read-only

A read-only access level is one in which no changes can be made. A read-only user can view settings, configurations, and so on, but can never make any changes. An account like this might be used to check the performance stats of a device. Read-only access is also usually the first level a user logs into before changing to a higher access-level mode.

Superuser

A superuser is the access level that grants the user full autonomy over the system. The superuser can add accounts, delete files, and configure any parameter on the system.

Other levels

Many products offer additional user levels that qualify somewhere between the access level of a superuser and a read-only user. Such an account might allow a user to change SLB parameters, but not system parameters. Another level might allow configuration of Ethernet port settings, but nothing else. Vendors typically have unique methods for user-access levels.

Redundancy

Redundancy as a concept is simple: if one device should fail, another will take its place and function, with little or no impact on operations as a whole. Just about every load-balancing product on the market has this capability, and certainly all of those featured in this book do.

There are several ways to achieve this functionality. Typically, two devices are implemented. A protocol is used by one device to check on its partner's health. In some scenarios, both devices are active and accept traffic, while in others, only one device is used while the other waits in case of failure.

Redundancy Roles

In redundancy, there is often an active-standby relationship. One unit, known as the active unit, takes on some or all of the functions, while another, the standby, waits to take on these functions. This is also often called the master/slave relationship.

In certain scenarios, both units can be masters of some functions and slaves of others, in order to distribute the load. In other cases, both are masters of all functions, sharing between the two. This is known as active-active redundancy.

Active-Standby Scenario

The active-standby redundancy scenario is the easiest to understand and implement. One device takes the traffic while the other waits in case of failure (see Figure 2-1).

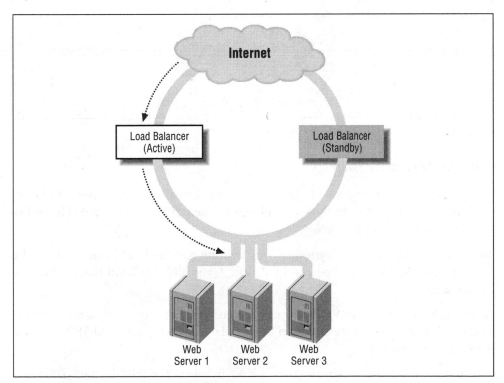

Figure 2-1. An active-standby redundancy scenario

If the second unit were to fail, the other device would have some way of determining that failure and would take over the traffic (see Figure 2-2).

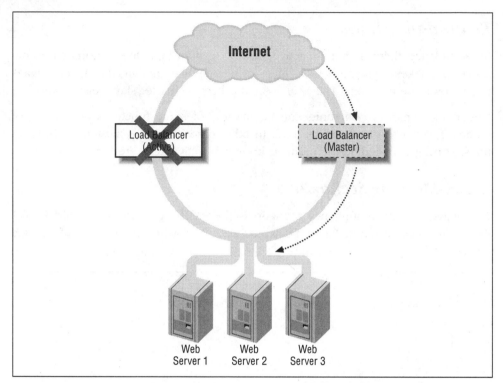

Figure 2-2. An active-standby failure scenario

Active-Active Scenario

There are several variations of the active-active scenario. In all cases, however, both units accept traffic. In the event of one of the devices failing, the other takes over the failed unit's functions.

In one variation, VIPs are distributed between the two load balancers to share the incoming traffic. VIP 1 goes to Load Balancer A and VIP 2 to Load Balancer B (see Figure 2-3).

In another variation, both VIPs answer on both load balancers, with a protocol circumventing the restriction that two load balancers may not hold the same IP address (see Figure 2-4).

As in all active-active scenarios, if one load balancer should fail, the VIP(s) will continue to answer on the remaining one. The other unit takes over all functions (see Figure 2-5).

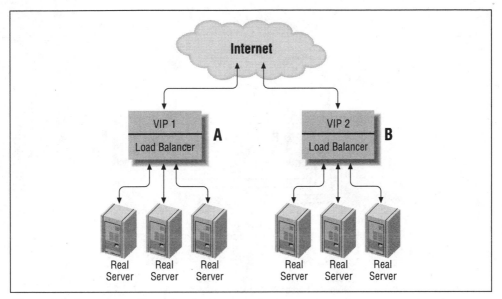

Figure 2-3. An active-active redundancy scenario

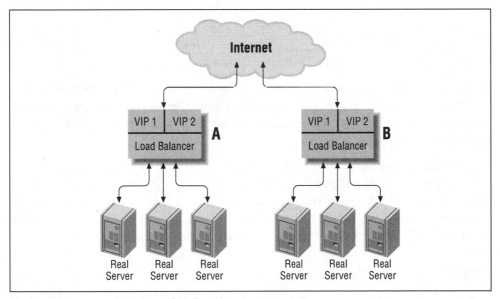

Figure 2-4. An active-active redundancy scenario variation

VRRP

Perhaps the most common redundancy protocol is the Virtual Router Redundancy Protocol (VRRP). It is an open standard, and devices claiming VRRP support conform to the specifications laid out in RFC 2338.

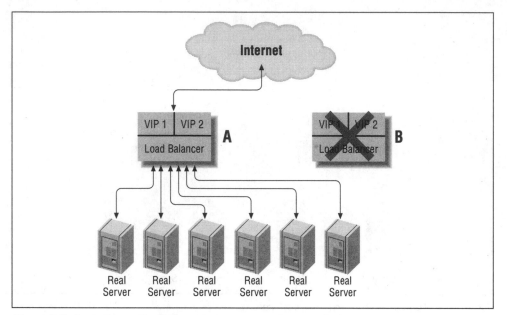

Figure 2-5. An active-active failure-recovery scenario

Each unit in a pair sends out packets to see if the other will respond. If the sending unit does not get a response from its partner, then the unit assumes that its partner is disabled and initiates taking over its functions, if any.

While it's not necessary to know the inner workings of the VRRP protocol, some details may come in handy. VRRP uses UDP port 1985 and sends packets to the multicast address 225.0.0.2. These details are useful when dealing with some types of IP-filtering or firewalling devices.

VRRP requires that the two units are able to communicate with each other. Should the two units become isolated from one another, each will assume the other unit is dead and take on "master" status. This circumstance can cause serious network problems because of IP-address conflicts and other network issues that occur when two units think they are both the active units in an active-standby situation.

xxRP

There are several proprietary versions of VRRP, each usually ending in "RP." Two examples are Extreme Network's Extreme Standby Router Protocol (ESRP) and Cisco's Hot Standby Routing Protocol (HSRP). While these protocols vary slightly from the standard, they all behave in essentially the same manner.

Fail-Over Cable

Another method for detecting unit failure between a pair of devices is provided by the fail-over cable. This method uses a proprietary "heartbeat" checking protocol running over a serial line between a pair of load balancers.

If this fail-over cable is disconnected, it causes both units to believe they are the only units available, and each takes on "master" status. This, as with the VRRP scenario, can cause serious network problems. Spanning-Tree Protocol (STP) is a protocol for Layer 2 redundancy that avoids bridging loops. STP sets a priority for a given port, and when multiple paths exist for traffic, only the highest-priority port is left active, with the rest being administratively shut down.

Stateful Fail-Over

One of the issues that a fail-over scenario presents (the "little" in little or no impact on network operations, as stated earlier) is if a device fails over, all of the active TCP connections are reset, and TCP sequence number information is lost, which results in a network error displayed on your browser. Also, if you are employing some form of persistence, that information will be reset as well (a bad scenario for a web-store type application). Some vendors have employed a feature known as "stateful fail-over," which keeps session and persistence information on both the active and standby unit. If the active unit fails, then the standby unit will have all of the information, and service will be completely uninterrupted. If done correctly, the end user will notice nothing.

Persistence

Also referred to as the "sticky," persistence is the act of keeping a specific user's traffic going to the same server that was initially hit when the site was contacted. While the SLB device may have several machines to choose from, it will always keep a particular user's traffic going to the same server. This is especially important in web-store type applications, where a user fills a shopping cart, and that information may only be stored on one particular machine. There are several ways to implement persistence, each with their advantages and drawbacks.

Service Checking

One of the tasks of an SLB device is to recognize when a server or service is down and take that server out of rotation. Also known as health checking, this can be performed a number of ways. It can be something as simple as a ping check, a port check, (to see if port 80 is answering), or even a content check, in which the web server is queried for a specific response. An SLB device will continuously run these service checks, usually at user-definable intervals.

Load-Balancing Algorithms

Depending on your specific needs, there are several methods of distributing traffic among a group of servers using a given metric. These are the mathematical algorithms programmed into the SLB device. They can run on top and in conjunction with any of the persistence methods. They are assigned to individual VIPs.

Provider Infrastructure

The networking infrastructure is composed of the networking components that give connectivity to the Internet, Extranet, or Intranet for your web servers. It connects them to the users of your services. This is usually done one of two ways: in a location controlled by the site or in a location maintained by a colocation/ hosting provider that specializes in hosting other companies' server infrastructures. Provider infrastructure also includes the facility that your site is housed in, whether it be your facility or the provider's facility.

Data Center

Whether your site is housed internally or at a colocation provider, your equipment is usually housed in type of space called a data center. Data center is a fairly general term, but it usually refers to an area with high security, environmental controls (usually air conditioning), nonwater-based fire suppression (such as Halon or FM200), and UPS power backup systems with generators on standby, among other things. Money is probably the determining factor in the level and quality of the data center environment, from Fort Knox conditions to (literally) someone's basement.

Leased Line

In a leased-line scenario, a site is housed internally with one or more leased-line connections from one or more providers. It can be as simple as a DSL line or as complicated as multiple OC3s running full BGP sessions to multiple providers. The advantage of this is that you have full control and access over your equipment. In Figure 2-6, we see a common leased-line scenario, where one location is connected to the Internet via two DS-3 (45 Mbps) lines from two separate providers. The site would probably run BGP on both lines, which is a protocol that allows redundancy in case a line from one provider goes down.

Colocation

Colocation is when you take your servers and equipment to a provider's location and house all your equipment there. Usually in racks or secure cages, your equipment

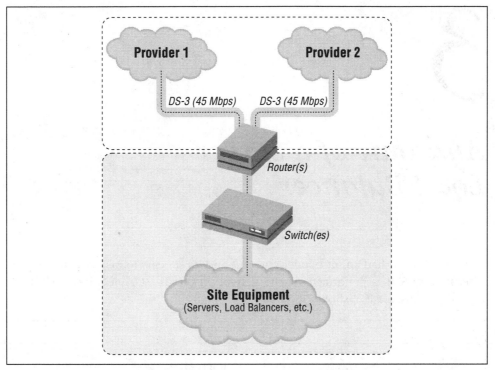

Figure 2-6. A leased-line scenario

sits on the colocation provider's property and is subject to its security, power, bandwidth, and environmental controls. The colocation provider typically provides the bandwidth through his or her own connectivity/backbone through a "network drop," usually an Ethernet connection (or multiple connections for redundancy). The advantage to colocation is that a colocation provider's bandwidth is usually more scalable than what you would have at your own facility. When you want more bandwidth from a colocation provider, you just take it, or upgrade your Ethernet lines, which don't take long to procure (a couple of days, depending on your provider). If you have leased lines to your own facility, it can take anywhere from 30 days to 6 months to get telco companies to add more bandwidth, such as T-1 (1.5 Mbps) or DS-3 (45 Mbps). Higher capacity lines usually take even longer.

Colocation is the typical route taken nowadays, mostly because of cost and scalability concerns. It's just easier and cheaper in most situations to let another company worry about the data center and connectivity. Its network connectivity is usually very complex, involving peering points, leased lines to other providers, sometimes even its own backbone. Usually, all a hosted site need concern itself with is the network drop from the provider. This will be the scenario discussed from here on in.

3

Anatomy of a Server Load Balancer

Now that you've had an introduction to SLB and its specific terms, this chapter will discuss how SLB is performed on the network level. To start, lets look at a fairly typical SLB installation, shown in Figure 3-1.

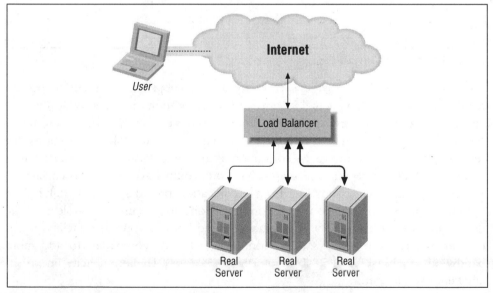

Figure 3-1. A typical SLB implementation

Traffic traverses from the user to the load balancer, to the real server, and then back out to the user. In this chapter I will dissect this path and see how the packets are manipulated to better understand how SLB works.

A Day in the Life of a Packet

As stated previously, SLB works by manipulating a packet before and (usually) after it reaches an actual server. This is typically done by manipulating the source or destination IP addresses of a Layer 3 IP packet in a process known as Network Address Translation (NAT).

In Figure 3-2, you see an IP packet sent from a source address of 208.185.43.202 destined for 192.168.0.200. This IP header is like the "To" and "From" portions of a letter sent through the post office. Routers use that information to forward the packets along on their journeys through the various networks.

| Source IP Address 208.185.43.202 | Destination IP Address 192.168.0.200 |

Figure 3-2. An IP packet header

One issue of great importance in dealing with SLB, and TCP/IP in general, is that when you send a packet to an IP, the packet needs to be returned with the same source address and destination address. In other words, when you send a packet to a destination, it has to be sent back from that destination, not from another IP altogether. If the packet does not come from the IP address it was sent to, the packet is dropped. This is not an issue with UDP-based packets, since UDP is a connectionless protocol. However, most SLB implementations involve web serving, which is TCP-based.

> Later in this book we will discuss two different types of SLB implementation strategies known as flat-based and NAT-based SLB. In reality, both of these implementations perform NAT, but in NAT-based SLB, the NAT part of the name refers to translating from one IP subnet to another.

To illustrate how SLB is accomplished, I'll follow a packet on its way in and out of a web server (see Figure 3-3). Let's take the example of a client IP address of 208. 185.43.202, a VIP address of 192.168.0.200, and a real server IP address of 192.168. 0.100. Since the VIP and the real server are both on the same subnet, this configuration is called "flat-based SLB" architecture. The details of flat-based architecture are discussed in Chapter 6.

To get to the site, a user inputs a URL, which translates into the VIP address of 192.168.0.200. The packet traverses the Internet with a source IP address of 208. 185.43.202 and a destination address of 192.168.0.200.

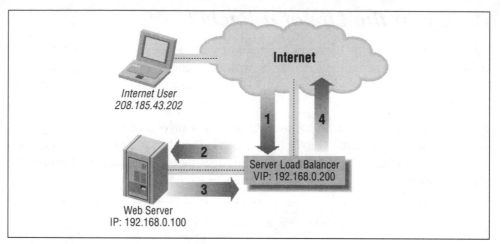

Figure 3-3. A day in the life of a packet

The load balancer takes the packet destined for 192.168.0.200 and, instead of responding to the request, rewrites the packet. For the packet to get to the real server, the destination address is rewritten with the address of the real server.

The source in step 2 is 208.185.43.202, and the destination is 192.168.0.100. The real server responds to the packet, and it is sent back to the user.

In step 3, the source becomes 192.168.0.100, and the destination becomes 208.185. 43.202, which presents a problem. The user will ignore a response from the IP address of 192.168.0.100, since the user never initiated a connection to that address; the user sent a packet to 192.168.0.200. The SLB unit solves this problem by being the default route of the real server and rewriting the packet before it is sent. The source address is rewritten to be the VIP, or 192.168.0.200.

The source in step 4 is 192.168.0.200 and the destination is 208.185.43.202. With that final rewrite, the packet completes its journey (see Table 3-1). To the user, it all seems like there is just one server, when in reality there could be several, even hundreds of real servers.

Table 3-1. SLB traffic manipulation

Step	Source IP	Destination IP
1	208.185.43.202	192.168.0.200
2	208.185.43.202	192.168.0.100
3	192.168.0.100	208.185.43.202
4	192.168.0.200	208.185.43.202

Direct Server Return

As introduced in Chapter 2, Direct Server Return (DSR) is a method of bypassing the load balancer on the outbound connection. This can increase the performance of the load balancer by significantly reducing the amount of traffic running through the device and its packet rewrite processes. DSR does this by skipping step 3 in the previous table. It tricks a real server into sending out a packet with the source address already rewritten to the address of the VIP (in this case, 192. 168.0.200). DSR accomplishes this by manipulating packets on the Layer 2 level to perform SLB. This is done through a process known as MAC Address Translation (MAT). To understand this process and how DSR works, let's take a look at some of the characteristics of Layer 2 packets and their relation to SLB.

MAC addresses are Layer 2 Ethernet hardware addresses assigned to every Ethernet network interface when they are manufactured. With the exception of redundancy scenarios, MAC addresses are generally unique and do not change at all with a given device. On an Ethernet network, MAC addresses guide IP packets to the correct physical device. They are just another layer of the abstraction of network workings.

DSR uses a combination of MAT and special real-server configuration to perform SLB without going through the load balancer on the way out. A real server is configured with an IP address, as it would normally be, but it is also given the IP address of the VIP. Normally you cannot have two machines on a network with the same IP address because two MAC addresses can't bind the same IP address. To get around this, instead of binding the VIP address to the network interface, it is bound to the loopback interface.

A loopback interface is a pseudointerface used for the internal communications of a server and is usually of no consequence to the configuration and utilization of a server. The loopback interface's universal IP address is 127.0.0.1. However, in the same way that you can give a regular interface multiple IP addresses (also known as IP aliases), loopback interfaces can be given IP aliases too. By having the VIP address configured on the loopback interface, we get around the problem of not having more than one machine configured with the same IP on a network. Since the VIP address is on the loopback interface, there is no conflict with other servers as it is not actually on a physical Ethernet network.

In a regular SLB situation, the web server or other service is configured to bind itself to the VIP address on the loopback interface, rather than to a real IP address. The next step is to actually get traffic to this nonreal VIP interface. This is where MAT comes in. As said before, every Ethernet-networked machine has a MAC address to identify itself on the Ethernet network. The load balancer takes the traffic on the VIP, and instead of changing the destination IP address to that of the real server (step 2 in Table 3-1), DSR uses MAT to translate the destination MAC address. The real server would normally drop the traffic since it doesn't have the VIP's IP address, but because the VIP address is configured on the loopback interface, we trick the server into accepting the traffic. The beauty of this process is that when the server responds and sends the traffic back out, the destination address is already that of the VIP, thus skipping step 3 of Table 3-1, and sending the traffic unabated directly to the client's IP.

Let's take another look at how this DSR process works in Table 3-2.

Table 3-2. The DSR process

Step	Source IP	Destination IP	MAC Address
1	208.185.43.202	192.168.0.200	Destination: 00:00:00:00:00:aa
2	208.185.43.202	192.168.0.200	Destination: 00:00:00:00:00:bb
3	192.168.0.200	208.185.43.202	Source: 00:00:00:00:00:bb

Included in this table are the MAC addresses of both the load balancer (00:00:00:00:00:aa) and the real server (00:00:00:00:00:bb).

As with the regular SLB example, 192.168.0.200 represents the site to which the user wants to go, and is typed into the browser. A packet traverses the Internet with a source IP address of 208.185.43.202 and a destination address of the VIP on the load balancer. When the packet gets to the LAN that the load balancer is connected to, it is sent to 192.168.0.200 with a MAC address of 00:00:00:00:aa.

In step 2, only the MAC address is rewritten to become the MAC address that the real server has, which is 00:00:00:00:00:bb. The server is tricked into accepting the packet and is processed by the VIP address configured on the loopback interface.

In step 3, the traffic is sent out to the Internet and to the user with the source address of the VIP, with no need to send it through the load balancer. Figure 3-4 shows the same process in a simplified diagram.

Web traffic has a ratio of about 1:8, which is one packet out for every eight packets in. If DSR is implemented, the workload of the load balancer can be reduced by a factor of 8. With streaming or download traffic, this ratio is even higher. There can easily be 200 or more packets outbound for every packet in, thus DSR can significantly reduce the amount of traffic with which the load balancer must contend.

The disadvantage to this process is that it is not always a possibility. The process requires some fairly interesting configurations on the part of the real servers and the server software running on them. These special configurations may not be possible with all operating systems and server software. This process also adds

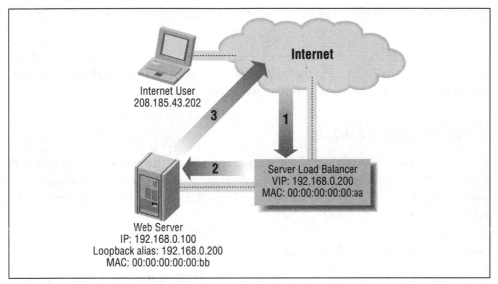

Figure 3-4. The DSR traffic path

complexity to a configuration, and added complexity can make a network architecture more difficult to implement. Also, any Layer 5–7 URL parsing or hashing
would not work because that process requires a synchronous data path in and out
of the load balancer. Cookie-based persistence would not work in most situations,
although it is possible.

Other SLB Methods

There are several other ways to perform network-based SLB. The way it is normally implemented is sometimes called "half-NAT," since either the source address
or the destination address of a packet is rewritten, but not both. A method known
as "full-NAT" also exists. Full-NAT rewrites the source and destination addresses at
the same time. A given scenario might look like the one in Table 3-3.

Table 3-3. Full-NAT SLB

Step	Source	Destination
1	208.185.43.202	192.168.0.200
2	10.0.0.1	10.0.0.100
3	10.0.0.100	10.0.0.1
4	192.168.0.200	208.185.43.202

In this situation, all source addresses, regardless of where the requests come from,
are set to one IP address. The downside to this is that full-NAT renders web logs

useless, since all traffic from the web server's point of view comes from one IP address.

A situation like this has limited uses in SLB and won't be discussed beyond this chapter. It can sometimes be useful for features such as proxy serving and cache serving, but for SLB, full-NAT is not generally used.

Under the Hood

SLB devices usually take one of two basic incarnations: the switch-based load balancer or the server-based load balancer. Each has its general advantages and drawbacks, but these greatly depend on how the vendor has implemented the technology.

Server-Based Load Balancers

Server-based load balancers are usually PC-based units running a standard operating system. Cisco's LocalDirector and F5's BIG-IP are both examples of server-based load balancers. SLB functions are performed by software code running on top of the network stack of the server's OS. Generally, the OS is an OEMed version of a commercial OS such as BSDI or a modified freeware OS such as Linux or FreeBSD. In a load balancer such as Cisco's LocalDirector, the entire OS is written by the manufacturer.

Server-based load balancers are typically easy to develop for because the coding resources for a widely used OS are easy to come by. This can help shorten code and new-feature turnaround, but it can also be a hindrance. With shorter code cycles, bugs can become more prevalent. This easy development cycle means that sever-based load balancers are typically flexible in what they can do. New features can be rolled out swiftly, and the machines themselves can take on new and creative ways of performance monitoring, as well as other tasks.

Switch-Based Load Balancers

Switch-based load balancers, also known as hardware-based load balancers, are devices that rely on Application Specific Integrated Circuit (ASIC) chips to perform the packet-rewriting functions. ASIC chips are much more specialized processors than their Pentium or PowerPC cousins. Pentium and PowerPC chips have a general instruction set to them, which enables a wide variety of software to be run, such as Quake III or Microsoft Word. An ASIC chip is a processor that removes several layers of abstraction from a task. Because of this specialization, ASIC chips often perform software tasks much faster and more efficiently than a general processor. The drawback to this is that the chips are very inflexible. If a new task is needed, then a new ASIC design may have to be built. However, the IP protocol has remained unchanged, so it's possible to burn those functions into an ASIC.

The Alteon and Cisco CSS lines of load-balancing switches, as well as Foundry's ServerIron series, are all examples of switch-based load balancers featured in this book.

Switch-based load balancers are typically more difficult to develop code for. They often run on proprietary architectures, or at least architectures with minimal development resources. Therefore, code comes out slower but is more stable.

The switch-based products are also usually faster. Their ASIC chips are more efficient than software alone. Typically, they also have internal-bandwidth backbones capable of handling a Gbps worth of traffic. PCs are geared more toward general I/O traffic and are not optimized for IP or packet traffic.

It All Depends

Again, it needs to be said that while there are certain trends in characteristics of the two main types of architectures, they do not necessarily hold true in every case. Performance, features, and stability are issues that can vary greatly from vendor to vendor. Therefore, it would be unfair to state that any given switch-based load balancer is a better performer than a PC-based load balancer, or that any PC-based load balancer has more features than a switch-based load balancer.

4

Performance Metrics

In this chapter, I will discuss the many facets of performance associated with SLB devices. There are many different ways to measure performance in SLB devices, and each metric has a different level of importance depending on the specific needs of a site. The metrics discussed in this chapter include:

- Connections per second
- Total concurrent connections
- Throughput (in bits per second)

Performance metrics are critical because they gauge the limit of your site's implementation.

Connections Per Second

As far as pure performance goes, this is probably the most important metric, especially with HTTP. Connections per second relates to the number of incoming connections an SLB device accepts in a given second. This is sometimes referred to as transactions per second or sessions per second, depending on the vendor. It is usually the limiting factor on any device, the first of any of the metrics to hit a performance limit. The reason this metric is so critical is that opening and closing HTTP connections is very burdensome on a network stack or network processor. Lets take a simplified look at the steps necessary to transfer one file via HTTP:

1. The client box initiates an HTTP connection by sending a TCP SYN packet destined for port 80 to the web server.

2. The web server sends an ACK packet back to the client along with an additional SYN packet.

3. The client sends back an ACK packet in response to the server's SYN request.

The beginning of a connection is known as the "three-way handshake." After the handshake is negotiated, data can pass back and forth. In the case of HTTP, this is usually a web page.

Now this process has quite a few steps for sending only 30 KB worth of data, and it strains a network device's resources. Setting up and tearing down connections is resource-intensive. This is why the rate at which a device can accomplish this is so critical.

If you have a site that generates a heavy amount of HTTP traffic in particular, this is probably the most important metric you should look for when shopping for an SLB device.

Total Concurrent Connections

Total concurrent connections is the metric for determining how many open TCP user sessions an SLB device can support. Usually, this number is limited by the available memory in an SLB device's kernel or network processor. The number ranges from infinity to only a few thousand, depending on the product. Most of the time, however, the limit is theoretical, and you would most likely hit another performance barrier before encountering the total available session number.

For UDP traffic, concurrent connections are not a factor, as UDP is a completely connectionless protocol. UDP traffic is typically associated with either streaming media or DNS traffic, although there are several other protocols that run on UDP. Most load balancers are capable of handling UDP protocols for SLB.

Throughput

Throughput is another important metric. Typically measured in bits per second, throughput is the rate at which an SLB device is able to pass traffic through its internal infrastructure. All devices have internal limiting factors based on architectural design, so it's important to know the throughput when looking for an SLB vendor. For instance, a few SLB vendors only support Fast Ethernet, thus limiting them to 100 Mbps (Megabits per second). In addition, some server-based products may not have processors and/or code fast enough to handle transfer rates over 80 Mbps.

While throughput is measured in bits per second, it is actually a combination of two different variables: packet size and packets per second. Ethernet packets vary in length, with a typical Maximum Transmittable Unit (MTU) of about 1.5 KB. If a particular piece of data is larger than 1.5 KB, then it is chopped up into 1.5 KB chunks for transport. The number of packets per second is really the most important factor a load balancer or any network device uses. The combination of this and packet size determines the bits per second. For example, an HTTP GET on a 100-byte text file will fit into one packet very easily. An HTTP GET on a 32 KB image file will result in the file being chopped into about 21 Ethernet packets, but each would have a full 1.5 KB payload. The bigger the payload, the more efficient use of resources. This is one of the main reasons why connections per second is such an important metric. Not only do connections per second cause quite a bit of overhead on just the initiation of a connection, but sites that experience high rates of connections per second typically have small payloads. Throughput can be calculated as follows:

Throughput = packet transmission rate × payload size

The 100 Mbps Barrier

As stated before, many SLB models are equipped with only Fast Ethernet interfaces, thus limiting the total throughput to 100 Mbps. While most users aren't necessarily concerned with pushing hundreds of Megs worth of traffic, many are concerned that while they push 50 Mbps today, they should be able to push 105 Mbps in the future.

To get around this, there are a couple of techniques available. One technique involves Fast EtherChannel, which binds two or more Fast Ethernet links into one link, combining the available bandwidth. This isn't the simplest solution by far, and there are limits to how Fast EtherChannel distributes traffic, such as when one portion of the link is flooded while another link is unused.

Another solution is the Direct Server Return (DSR) technology discussed in Chapters 2 and 3. Since DSR does not involve the outbound traffic passing the SLB device, which is typically the majority of a site's traffic, the throughput requirements of an SLB device are far less. At that point, the limiting factor would become the overall connectivity of the site.

The simplest solution to this problem is using Gigabit Ethernet (GigE) on the load balancers. The costs of GigE are dropping to more affordable levels, and it's a great way to aggregate large amounts of traffic to Fast Ethernet-connected servers. Since the limit is 1 Gbps (Gigabit per second), there is plenty of room to grow a 90 Mbps site into a 190 Mbps site and beyond. Getting beyond 1 Gbps is a challenge that future SLB products will face.

Traffic Profiles

Each site's traffic characteristics are different, but there are some patterns and similarities that many sites do share. There are three typical traffic patterns that I have identified and will go over in this section. HTTP, FTP/Streaming, and web store traffic seem to be fairly typical as far as traffic patterns go. Table 4-1 lists these patterns and their accompanying metrics. Of course, the traffic pattern for your site may be much different. It is critical to identify the type or types of traffic your sites generate to better design your site, secure your site, and tune its performance.

Table 4-1. The metrics matrix

Traffic pattern	Most important metric	Second most important metric	Least important metric
HTTP	Connections per second	Throughput	Total sustained connections
FTP/Streaming	Throughput	Total sustained connections	Connections per second
Web store	Total sustained connections	Connections per second	Throughput

HTTP

HTTP traffic is generally bandwidth-intensive, though it generates a large amount of connections per second. With HTTP 1.0, a TCP connection is opened for every object, whether it be an HTML file, an image file (such as a GIF or JPEG), or text file. A web page with 10 objects on it would require 10 separate TCP connections to complete. The HTTP 1.1 standard makes things a little more efficient by making one connection to retrieve several objects during a given session. Those 10 objects on the example page would be downloaded in one continuous TCP connection, greatly reducing the work the load balancer and web server would need to do. HTTP is still fairly inefficient as far as protocols go, however. Web pages and their objects are typically kept small to keep download times small, usually with a 56K modem user in mind (a user will likely leave your site if the downloads take too long). So web pages generally don't contain much more than 70 or 80 KB worth of data in them. Now, that number greatly varies depending on the site, but it is still a relatively small amount of data.

FTP/Streaming

FTP and streaming traffic are very similar in their effects on networks. Both involve one initial connection (or in the case of streaming, which often employs UDP, no connection) and a large amount of data transferred. The rate of FTP/streaming initial connections will always remain relatively small compared to the amount of data transferred. One FTP connection could easily involve a download of a Megabyte or more worth of data. This can saturate networks, and the 100 Mbps limit is usually the one to watch.

Web Stores

Web stores are where the money is made on a site. This is the money that usually pays the bills for the network equipment, load balancers, and salaries (and also this book!), so this traffic must be handled with special care. Speed is of the utmost importance for this type of traffic; users are less likely to spend money on sites that are too slow for them. This type of traffic does not generally involve a large amount of bandwidth, nor does it involve a large amount of connections per second (unless there is a media-related event, such as a TV commercial). Sustained connections are important, though, considering that a site wants to support as many customers as possible.

Stateful redundancy

One critical feature to this type of profile, as opposed to the others, is the redundancy information kept between load balancers. This is known as stateful redundancy. Any TCP session and persistence data that one load balancer has, the other should have to minimize the impact of a fail-over, which is typically not a concern of noninteractive sites that are largely static. Cookie table information and/or TCP sessions need to be mirrored to accomplish this. Other profiles may not require this level of redundancy, but web stores usually do.

The Wall

When dealing with performance on any load-balancing device, there is a concept that I refer to as "the wall." The wall is a point where the amount of traffic being processed is high enough to cause severe performance degradation. Response time and performance remain fairly constant as traffic increases until the wall is reached, but when that happens, the effect is dramatic. In most cases, hitting the wall means slower HTTP response times and a leveling out of traffic. In extreme cases, such as an incredibly high amount of traffic, there can be unpredictable and strange behavior. This can include reboots, lock-ups (which do not allow the redundant unit to become the master), and kernel panics. Figure 4-1 shows the sharp curve that occurs when the performance wall is hit.

Additional Features

Of course, as you add features and capabilities to a load balancer, it is very likely that its performance may suffer. It all depends on how the load balancer is designed and the features that you are employing.

Load balancers don't generally respond any slower as you add features. However, adding features will most likely lower the upper limit of performance degradation.

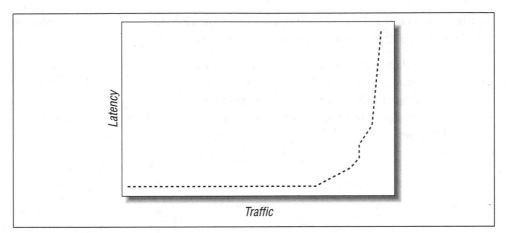

Figure 4-1. The performance barrier

For instance, if a load balancer can push 90 Mbps and no latency with just Layer 4 running, it may be able to push only 45 Mbps with URL parsing and cookie-based persistence enabled. The reason is that in Layer 5–7, much more (or even all) of the packet must be inspected. Doing this can be very CPU-intensive. Whether parsing the URL or reading the cookie in the packet, it's much more than just rewriting the IP header info.

Switch-based versus server-based performance degradation

The amount of performance degradation observed with the addition of functionality also greatly depends on the way the load balancer is engineered. In Chapter 3, I went over the differences between switch-based and server-based load balancers.

With server-based load balancers, this degradation is very linear as you add functions. The more the processor has to do, the lower the amount of traffic a load balancer can process with acceptable speed.

With switch-based load balancers, this is not necessarily the case. ASIC chips are employed to handle the network processing. Some vendors have developed ASIC chips to handle the functions of Layer 5 processing, resulting in a more distributed architecture with some components handling Layer 4, others handling Layer 5, and so on. Other switch-based vendors rely on ASICs for their Layer 4 functions and a general processor for the Layer 5–7 functions. The performance characteristics of each of these components can vary greatly.

The Alteon series of load balancers, for example, have dedicated pairs of processors for each port on their switches. Each set of processors has a CPU and memory, and is capable of independent handling of the traffic associated with that particular port. The Alteon 8.0 series and later also has a feature called Virtual

Matrix Architecture (VMA), which distributes network load to all the processors on a switch, even if they don't have traffic flowing through them.

In the end, it depends quite a bit on how a load balancer is coded and designed, and the features that it uses. These characteristics change from vendor to vendor and usually from model to model. It's important to know the type of traffic you are likely to run through the load balancer to understand how to plan for performance and potential growth needs.

II

Practice
and Implementation
of Server Load Balancing

5

Introduction to Architecture

Ask any hardcore networking gurus about network design, and they'll tell you that it is an art—and they are absolutely right. This chapter is an introduction to both the form and the function of a given network infrastructure with SLB. Like all engineering endeavors, there is a difference between adequacy and excellence, and that difference is often subtle.

When designing your SLB implementation, or any other network implementation, you should keep in mind the same design aspects that you would with any other engineering task. Such aspects include:

*   Simplicity
*   Functionality
*   Elegance

Inversely, you should avoid several aspects:

*   Complexity
*   Fanciness
*   Irrelevance

You are looking for the best, easiest, most elegant, and most cost-effective way to meet all of your requirements. Whether the requirements are spanning a river, a transatlantic flight, or SLB, the process is the same. When looking for a solution to fulfill all of a site's engineering requirements, always look for the simplest solution available.

One of the worst traps I see network designers fall into is trying to be fancy. They might think they are being clever by using a specific feature where it needn't be used, or a special configuration that garners little or no additional functionality.

They might revel in their own glory, but that's where the glory stops. Often, configurations like that become overly complex and unmanageable. When it comes down to crunch time, it's the least-complicated installation that survives.

Why do something in a convoluted manner when you can do it in an easy manner? Why include something that has no connection to what you are trying to accomplish? A colorful bow on a load balancer would merely be pretty, while color-coded Cat 5 cabling with a color-denoting function would be both aesthetically pleasing and extremely useful. Why throw a bunch of components together with no forethought of their interaction when you can compile the components in a logical and ordered way? You could go out and buy a router, a Layer 2/3 switch, and a load balancer, hook them all together and realize you probably didn't need a router when you have a Layer 2/3 switch (a switch that includes router functionality). Always keep in mind the age-old engineering adage of KISS: Keep It Simple Stupid!

Keeping it simple and elegant will reap untold benefits for your configuration. It will lower your costs by reducing the amount of necessary equipment. It will simplify maintenance because a simple site is much easier to upkeep than a complex installation. It will also come in handy during a crisis situation, simplifying the troubleshooting that needs to be done.

Architectural Details

Most of the people with whom I've spoken say that the most confusing parts of understanding SLB aren't the concepts or functions. The most confusing part of SLB is how load balancers fit into a given network infrastructure. There are several different ways to implement SLB units in a given network infrastructure, with many vendors supporting different methods. This can seem quite confusing, but all of the different ways SLB can be configured in a network can be boiled down to those shown in in Figure 5-1.

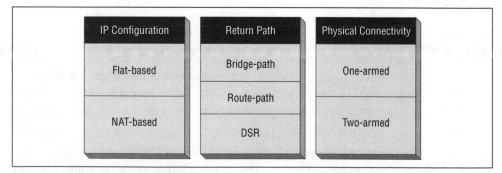

Figure 5-1. An SLB implementation matrix

The first column represents the layout of the IP topology. For flat-based SLB, the VIPs and real servers are on the same subnet. For NAT-based SLB, the VIPs and the real servers are on separate subnets. The second column represents how the traffic is directed to the load balancers on the way from the server to the Internet. Bridge-path means the load balancer is acting as a bridge, being in the Layer 2 path of outbound traffic. Route-path means the load balancer is acting as a router, being in the Layer 3 path of outbound traffic. Direct Server Return (DSR) is when the servers are specially configured to bypass the load balancer completely on the way out.

Virtually every load-balancing implementation can be classified by using one characteristic from each column. Most load-balancing products support several of the possible configurations, which can become quite confusing. This matrix greatly simplifies categorizing a given installation or planned installation. However, not all combinations are possible, as shown in Figure 5-1. Some don't make any sense from an architectural standpoint, and some just aren't feasible.

IP Address Configuration: Flat-Based SLB Versus NAT-Based SLB

These two concepts will be the basis for the next two chapters, as well as the basis for configuration strategies involving some of the different load balancers discussed in later chapters. Each way has its own advantages and strengths, and a site's particular requirements will be the determining factor for which to use.

As you can see with the flat-based SLB architecture shown in Figure 5-2, VIPs and nodes are on the same subnets. This can be done with either a bridging-path or route-path SLB method.

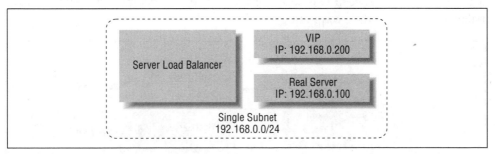

Figure 5-2. Flat-based SLB architecture

With the NAT-based SLB architecture shown in Figure 5-3, the load balancer sits on two separate subnets and usually two different VLANs. The load balancer is the default gateway of the real servers, and therefore employs the route-path SLB method. Bridging-path SLB will not work with NAT-based SLB.

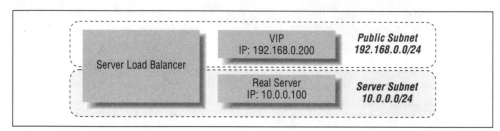

Figure 5-3. NAT-based SLB architecture

Return Traffic Management: Bridging-Path Versus Routing-Path Versus DSR

Most of the configurations I discuss will use route-path SLB rather than bridging-path. There are a number of reasons for this, first and foremost being that route-path is typically simpler to implement. In conjunction with the one-armed or two-armed physical connectivity, any inherent topology and redundancy issues are much easier to resolve. Bridging-path SLB works only with a flat-based SLB implementation, while route-path SLB works with either flat-based or NAT-based SLB.

With bridging-path SLB, you run into some deployment limitations. Since bridging-path SLB works on the Layer 2 level, there can be only one Layer 2 path on which traffic flows, thus limiting your load-balancer installation to one redundant pair (one does not forward Layer 2 traffic as a standby unit). If there is more than one pair, there is more than one Layer 2 path, resulting in either a bridging loop (very bad) or Layer 2 devices on the network shutting off one or more of the load-balancer ports.

In Figure 5-4, you can see how bridging works with SLB. The load balancer acts as a Layer 2 bridge between two separate LANs. The packets must traverse the load balancer in and on their ways out.

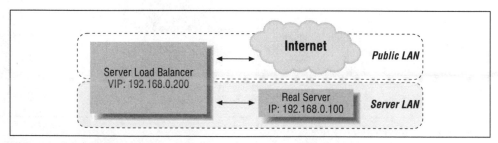

Figure 5-4. Bridging-path SLB architecture

With route-path SLB (shown in Figure 5-5), the load balancer is the default route of the real servers. It works like a router by forwarding packets.

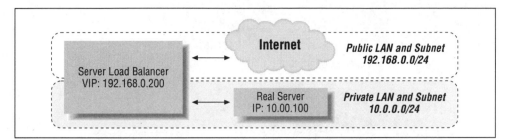

Figure 5-5. NAT-based, route-path SLB architecture

One-Armed Versus Two-Armed

There are a number of possible configurations with flat-based and NAT-based SLB architectures. However, in this book, one-armed is used only with flat-based SLB and two-armed, only with NAT-based SLB. There are a number of reasons for this. With flat-based, using a one-armed method means using the route-path method. With NAT-based SLB, security is better served by using two separate VLANs for the outside and internal networks.

With a one-armed configuration (shown in Figure 5-6), there is only one connection from the load balancer to the network infrastructure. This is perfect for flat-based SLB, since it involves real servers and VIPs on the same subnet and LAN. With NAT-based SLB, it is possible to have both the outside and internal networks on the same link, but that creates a security hazard and, thus, should be avoided.

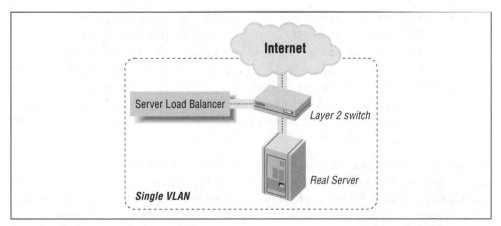

Figure 5-6. One-armed SLB configuration

With a two-armed configuration (shown in Figure 5-7), two separate links connect to two separate VLANs on two different subnets. This is the perfect configuration for NAT-based SLB, as it provides two links on separate networks. This also works great when using NAT-based SLB as part of a security scheme.

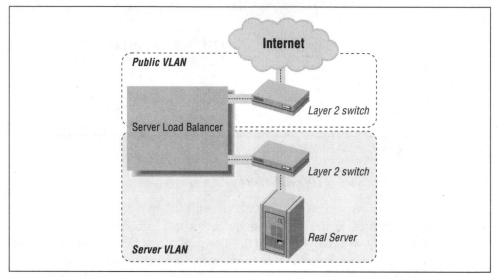

Figure 5-7. Two-armed SLB configuration

Two-armed is also used for bridge-path topologies, since the load balancer bridges two separate LANs. It isn't possible to achieve a one-armed configuation with bridge-path, since the load balancer bridges between two separate LANs.

Infrastructure

Infrastructure deals with how the load balancers and other components are connected to the outside world. There are a variety of possible infrastructure scenarios, such as ISPs, colocation data centers, in-house hosting off of leased lines, and many more. Infrastructure's primary purpose is to provide connectivity to the outside world and to the Internet. In addition, it often tries to provide a measure of redundancy in case any device or network link fails. Capacity is also an issue with infrastructure, as it tries to assure that there will be enough bandwidth available to service any need.

For any networked infrastructure to work, it needs to have two basic components: Layer 3 connectivity and Layer 2 aggregation. A Layer 3 router (or a pair for redundancy) is needed to home the network, and from which provide the IP connectivity, to the Internet and the outside world. There is also a Layer 2 infrastructure that aggregates this IP traffic through Ethernet, connecting the servers, load balancers, routers, and so on. In most infrastructure situations, there is redundancy for the Layer 2 and Layer 3 portions as well.

There are several ways in which to build an Internet-connectivity infrastructure. The following sections discuss a few of the more popular scenarios you may encounter when dealing with SLB, which is usually in some sort of hosting or colocation center. This is significant because how the infrastructure is designed affects how a load balancer is connected to a network and how the load balancer's redundancy scheme is implemented.

Four Pack

When a site has it's own dedicated routers and switches, a simple setup known as a "four pack" is commonly used (see Figure 5-8). It's called the four pack because it utilizes four network devices in a redundant configuration: two switches and two routers.

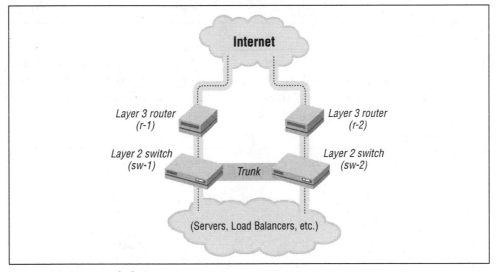

Figure 5-8. Four-pack design

Each switch is connected to a router to provide redundancy. VRRP or a similar Layer 3 redundancy protocol (such as Cisco's HSRP) runs between the two routers over the trunk link between the two switches. With a trunk between the two switches, it doesn't matter to which switch a device is connected, as it will still have connectivity (see Figure 5-9).

This scenario can suffer the failure of any one component. With VRRP running between the routers, if sw-1 were to die with r-1 as the active router, then r-2 would no longer be able to get to r-1. Since the health-check packets would not be answered, r-2 would become active and traffic would flow through sw-2.

The most common architectural error in the planning/design phase of a network occurs in how Layer 3 devices connect to Layer 2 devices (see Figure 5-10). When diagramming networks, designers have tendencies to interconnect as many devices

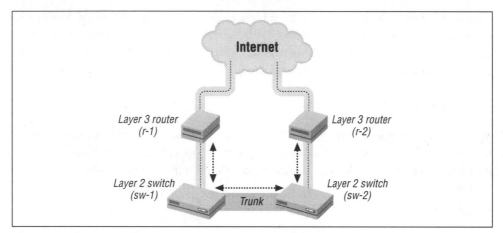

Figure 5-9. Four-pack flow

as possible, such as routers and switches. r-1 would have a link to both sw-1 and sw-2, and r-2 would have a link to sw-1 and sw-2 so as to provide added redundancy. Unfortunately, there aren't many routers that provide multiple Layer 2 ports on given interfaces.

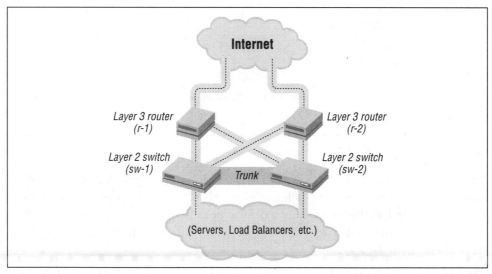

Figure 5-10. Four pack with cross-connects

While it is a good idea to cross-connect, it's often not possible.

Six Pack

If a network installation is housed at a colocation-style data center, chances are that you are connecting into its switch-router infrastructure. If this is the case, you'll probably need your own Layer 2 switches, but you will not need a router since the colocation company would provide this. Since it's much more cost effective to aggregate several clients off of a router port rather than dedicate a port to each customer, most providers use Layer 2 switches to distribute router-port traffic (see Figure 5-11). A client's Layer 2 switch would plug directly into the provider's Layer 2 switch, resulting in a configuration known as the "six pack" (two routers, two colocation provider switches, and two client switches). VRRP or similar protocols provide the redundancy on the routers.

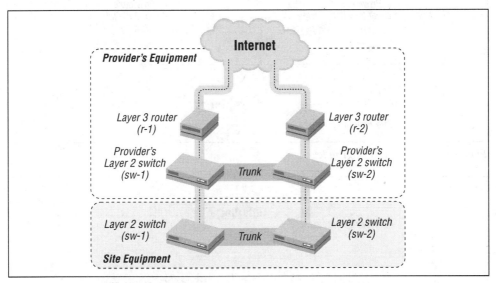

Figure 5-11. Six-pack design

To prevent a bridging loop (shown in Figure 5-12), some form of port blocking must be done on one of the ports to prevent multiple Layer 2 paths from existing. Spanning-Tree Protocol (STP) is a protocol that can take care of this automatically. Each port has a cost associated with it, with the lowest cost being preferred. If STP detects multiple paths, it shuts off all but the highest priority port (with the lowest number). It can be set up on the provider's end, the site's end, or both. Figure 5-13 shows an example of STP on the provider's right switch blocking the path between the provider's right switch and the site's right switch.

Multipurpose Devices

It is now possible—and even advantageous—to merge two or more typically separate functions into one. For example, a multitude of Layer 2/3 switches on the market incorporate the port capacity and Layer 2 functionality of a switch with the Layer 3 routing functions of a router. With the switch-based load balancers, incorporating Layer 4/5–7 with Layer 2/3 functionality is also possible. For the purposes

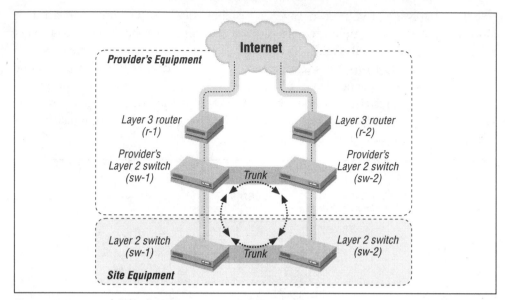

Figure 5-12. Six-pack bridging loop

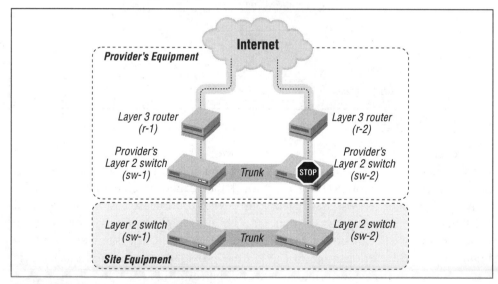

Figure 5-13. Six pack with STP blocking

of this book, however, I'll keep devices and their layered functions separate. For example, a Layer 2 device will be only a Layer 2 device. This is to keep things simple and easy to follow. This is not to say that combining them is not possible— or even not advantageous—but that they are simpler to understand when kept separate.

Cast of Characters

To keep things simple, several network components appear throughout the rest of this book. Components such as web servers and IP addresses remain constant, even though the topology or products may change. This keeps things easy to follow and allows for comparisons between different topologies and products. Every show needs its cast, so let me introduce you to the players.

Server Load Balancers

Since this book is about server load balancing, I am going to need load balancers. I will need two devices, as I am going to incorporate the high-availability functions. I call these load balancers lb-1 and lb-2, regardless of the vendors they represent.

Networks

Since load balancers are network-based, I need networks to configure them. So that O'Reilly & Associates, Inc. and I don't receive email from angry network administrators regarding their network IPs, I use private IP address space defined in RFC 1918. These are not publicly routed IP addresses, so anyone can use them for his own internal private network. These networks include:

    10.0.0.0–10.255.255.255
    172.16.0.0–172.16.255.255
    192.168.0.0–192.168.255.255

I use a /24 (256 IP addresses) worth of these nonrouted IPs in the example network designs. A block of IP addresses is called a netblock, which is just another word for a subnet.

Outside network

192.168.0.0/24 represents a publicly accessible and routable Class C worth of IP address space. This is the type of network on which a load-balanced VIP would be configured. As far as Layer 2 VLANs are concerned, the outside network is referred to as VLAN 1. Remember, while using this nonrouted netblock to represent a public network, your individual IP addresses depend on your network or network provider.

Internal network

10.0.0.0/24 represents a nonrouted IP address range used for some of the network topologies that I discuss later. Nonrouted IP addresses are advantageous because they provide an extra layer of security by making the servers difficult or impossible to access from the Internet. If a hacker is unable to reach your servers, she is unable to hack them. Even in your own network configuration, where the outside network consists of real IP addresses, the internal network is still composed of the nonrouted private RFC 1918 addresses (though not necessarily the subnet specified).

Web Servers

Since I am talking about implementing Server Load Balancing, I need servers to load balance. I call these web servers, since web serving is the most common use of SLB. However, SLB can be used with FTP, SMTP, POP3, media streaming, and many other network-based protocols.

The servers are given the prefix of ws (web server) and are known as ws-1, ws-2, ws-3, etc. They are assigned IP addresses from either the outside or internal network, depending on the network topology. When necessary, each web server has a network configuration table (see Table 5-1), which tells how to configure the basic IP stack of each device. Included is the default toute for the web server, which is crucial to the operation of SLB because it controls the flow of outbound traffic.

Table 5-1. Web server configuration

Server name	IP address	Subnet mask	Default gateway
ws-1	10.0.0.100	255.255.255.0	10.0.0.1

Routers

A redundant pair of routers provides connectivity to the outside world. VRRP (or HSRP with Cisco routers) runs between the routers to provide high availability in case one should fail. A pair of Layer 2 switches, discussed next, aggregates the Internet traffic. The routers are named r-1 and r-2. They are configured as shown in Table 5-2.

Table 5-2. Router configuration

Router	IP address	Subnet mask	VRRP shared address
r-1	192.168.0.2	255.255.255.0	192.168.0.1
r-2	192.168.0.3	255.255.255.0	192.168.0.1

Each router has an individual IP address and a shared VRRP address. The IP address is active on only one router at a time, thus having the same active-standby scenario that server load balancers do. Should a router fail, the IP would be picked up by the standby unit.

Switches

In all the network scenarios, a pair of Layer 2 switches is employed. Switches are the network devices that interconnect all of the devices (routers, server load balancers, servers, etc.) to aggregate the traffic. Since we are talking high availability, we employ a pair for redundancy. We use spanning-tree protocol to provide this Layer 2 redundancy. We call the switches sw-1 and sw-2. They can be configured with IPs on the network, but this isn't necessary. Given that most switches only support telnet (as opposed to an encrypted protocol such as SSH or Kerberos) and the given security implications, we leave them without IPs for now. Your own specific network needs will decide how to network them safely.

6

Flat-Based SLB Network Architecture

A flat-based SLB network architecture is, by definition, any SLB network implementation where the IPs of the VIPs and the IPs of the real servers are on the same subnet. It is named for the flatness of the network architecture because all the network components are on a single subnet.

Implementation

Flat-based is the simpler of the two SLB methods, the other method being NAT-based SLB. Flat-based works on a single subnet without translation into another subnet. While it is true that NAT is performed in most SLB scenarios (the only SLB scenario where NAT is not performed is DSR), since the load balancer isn't translating from one subnet to another, this method is not referred to as NAT.

Figure 6-1 shows the basic premise of flat-based SLB with simple connectivity into the Layer 2 infrastructure and the same subnet IP scheme. There are a few variations of flat-based SLB, but this is a simple and accurate representation.

Why Flat-Based?

There are several advantages to using the flat-based network, the main one being its simplicity. Flat-based is easier to manage, visualize, and design around, which keeps in line with the KISS philosophy.

Access to and from the outside network is always a concern with SLB, and with networks in general. With flat-based SLB, the servers have access to the outbound to the network without any special configurations such as reverse-NATs. There also isn't any extra configuration needed to access the web servers individually. Most sites have an administrative need to view each server separately from the load-balanced VIP, which isn't a problem for flat-based SLB.

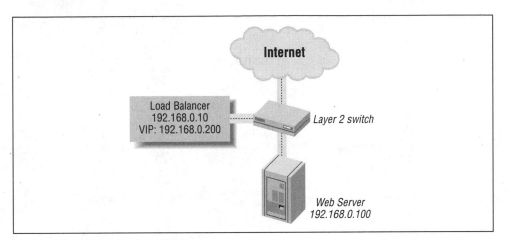

Figure 6-1. Simple, flat-based SLB

Flat-based SLB is ideal when a firewall has been implemented in front of the load balancers to take care of security requirements. While NAT-based is sometimes used as an additional security measure, when a firewall is present those measures are not required.

Flat-based SLB is also ideal for use with DSR. The load balancers can hang off the Layer 2 infrastructure, take the inbound traffic, and the outbound traffic flows right back out through the router or firewall. While DSR is possible with NAT-based SLB, it requires more equipment and is much more complicated to implement.

Streaming and FTP applications are often better served with flat-based SLB. One reason for this is that flat-based is ideal for DSR and, given the high traffic ratios (such as 200 packets out for every packet in), DSR can save quite a bit of resources on the load balancer by not having it process the 200 packets out, but only the 1 packet in. Also, some types of streaming applications don't handle NAT very well and need to have publicly routed IP addresses for the servers.

Route-Path, Bridge-Path, and DSR

Flat-based SLB can work equally easily with the route-path, bridge-path, and DSR methods of return-path. In Figure 6-2 we see a very typical installation (one used many times in the product configuration guides later in this book) involving route-path.

This is a flat-based, route-path, one-armed architecture. The load balancers are the default routes for the servers, even though they are on the same subnet as the router and are one-armed to the Layer 3 infrastructure. This ensures that the packets flow through the load balancer on the way out. To implement DSR on all or a just a portion of the site, only a configuration change is needed. Topology changes are not necessary.

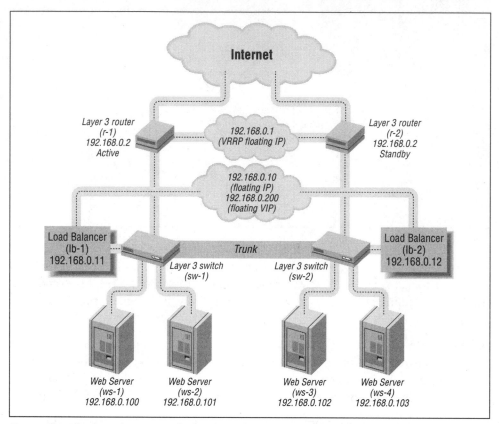

Figure 6-2. Flat-based, route-path, one-armed SLB

In Figure 6-3, we see a flat-based configuration using bridge-path instead of route-path. In this situation, the load balancers are in the Layer 2 path of the traffic flow.

Some products support only bridge-path, others support route-path, and a few products support both methods. There are several advantages to using the route-path method, including the ability to have several load balancers operating on a network. With the bridge-path method, only one pair of load balancers can be utilized. Any more load balancer sets may create a Layer 2 bridging loop. Also, DSR does not work with bridge-path, as the load balancer is in the Layer 2 path. Since there can be only one Layer 2 path (more than one Layer 2 path would create a nasty bridging loop), it's not possible to bypass the load balancer on the way out.

There are variations on the basic implementations of flat-based SLB, but for the most part, they conform to the previous examples. To decide on the best method, it's best to look at your overall needs and requirements, as well as the capabilities of the product.

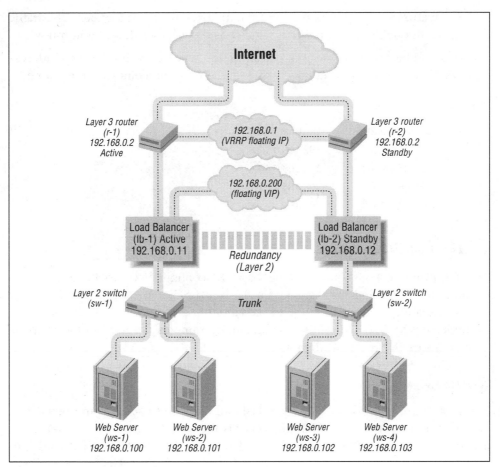

Figure 6-3. Flat-based, bridge-path, two-armed SLB

Traffic Flow

To understand how flat-based SLB works, let's take the example of a user with an IP address of 208.185.43.202. Table 6-1 illustrates the changes in IP source and destination addresses. The process takes four steps:

1. The user initiates an HTTP connection by typing the host name of vip-1 (192. 168.0.200) into the browser. The connection goes to the load balancer.

2. The load balancer takes the packet and rewrites the destination address, leaving the source address alone. The load balancer decides which server to send the connection to, and changes the destination address to 192.168.0.100, which would be the web server ws-1.

3. The web server responds and sends traffic back to 208.185.43.202. The traffic passes through the load balancer, since it is the web server's default route.

4. The load balancer rewrites the packet on the way out with the source address 192.168.0.200. The packet travels back to the user and completes the journey.

Table 6-1. Packet translation

Step	Source IP address	Destination IP address
1	208.185.43.202	192.168.0.200
2	208.185.43.202	192.168.0.100
3	192.168.0.100	208.185.43.202
4	192.168.0.200	208.185.43.202

Flat-Based Setup

The following sections outline some basic IP configurations to be used as an example for setup and installation of a flat-based SLB network. The redundancy and wiring are typical for this type of scenario, but are by no means the only way to implement an SLB site. These configuration examples are used in the chapters involving specific vendor configuration.

Routers

The routers are set up in a redundant fashion. Each unit backs up the other unit. One unit is the active unit, while the other is the standby. In Table 6-2, r-1 is the active unit with a VRRP priority of 200, while r-2 is the standby with a VRRP priority of 100.

Table 6-2. Router network configuration

Unit	r-1 (active)	r-2 (standby)
IP address	192.168.0.2	192.168.0.3
Subnet mask	255.255.255.0	255.255.255.0
VRRP IP address	192.168.0.1	192.168.0.1
VRRP priority	200	100

SLB Units

The SLB units in Table 6-3 are configured on the same subnet as the routers and web servers. They each have their own IP addresses, as well as a shared IP address for redundancy. The active unit (determined through VRRP, fail-over cable, or some other method) is the unit with the shared IP address, while the other unit waits to take the IP if the active unit should fail. They each have a single connection to the Layer 2 infrastructure.

Table 6-3. SLB network configuration

Unit	lb-1 (active)	lb-2 (standby)
IP address	192.168.0.11	192.168.0.12
Subnet mask	255.255.255.0	255.255.255.0
Shared address	192.168.0.10	192.168.0.10
Default route	192.168.0.1	192.168.0.1

Web Servers

While the web servers are on the same subnet as the routers, their default route is the load balancer's shared IP (see Table 6-4). This is so that traffic is rewritten on the way back out to the Internet.

Table 6-4. Web server network configuration

Unit	ws-1	ws-2	ws-3	ws-4
IP address	192.168.0.100	192.168.0.101	192.168.0.102	192.168.0.103
Subnet mask	255.255.255.0	255.255.255.0	255.255.255.0	255.255.255.0
Default route	192.168.0.10	192.168.0.10	192.168.0.10	192.168.0.10
Service and port	HTTP:80	HTTP:80	HTTP:80	HTTP:80

VIPs

The VIP is configured with a publicly routable IP address and this is the address the Internet uses to access the load-balanced site (see Table 6-5). Since the individual web servers are on the same subnet, you can access them directly without involving extra VIPs configured on the load balancers.

Table 6-5. VIP configuration

VIP	vip-1
IP address	192.168.0.200
Subnet mask	255.255.255.0
Service and port	HTTP:80
Real servers active	ws-1, ws-2, ws-3, ws-4

Redundancy

Flat-based SLB can use either route-path or bridge-path, so redundancy can occur on Layer 2 or Layer 3, depending on the method implemented. When using route-path, a Layer 2 redundancy is required. STP is almost never used since it can take 10 seconds or more to react. Typically, a proprietary variation of a hot-standby protocol is used, which quickly switches between active and standby units (in seconds or milliseconds), while still protecting a network against a bridging loop.

Security

Security measures are critical for flat-based SLB implementations because the load balancer does not usually have direct control over traffic destined for the servers. Without a firewall or other packet-filtering scheme, servers and load balancers—as well as VIPs and real servers on the same subnet—are open to malicious attack. This is not an acceptable security model for most sites, so you must find a way to protect your web server from hacking or attack.

One way to protect individual web servers is to place a firewall between the Internet-connected routers and the load balancers. A firewall would provide the packet filtering, stateful inspection, intrusion detection, and other measures necessary to adequately protect the network. Figure 6-4 shows an example of this security scheme involving flat-based SLB and a redundant set of firewalls.

One drawback of most firewall products is that they often have a traffic limit of about 70 to 80 Mbps, depending greatly on the firewall itself and on the type of traffic generated (streaming versus HTTP traffic, for instance). If the firewall product itself is not the limit, then the 100 Mbps Fast Ethernet interface could be, since many firewalls today do not have Gigabit Ethernet. This creates a potential bottleneck in an architecture that could otherwise easily support hundreds of Mbps worth of traffic.

Access lists on a router that connects the network to the load balancer are another option, but in hosting environments, it is often impossible to implement ACLs on a provider's equipment. Also, ACLs may not fulfill all of a site's security requirements.

Firewall Load Balancing (FWLB) is another solution. FWLB involves distributing the network load among a group of firewalls, in much the same manner that SLB distributes load among several servers. The drawback is that FWLB has a fairly complicated setup, requiring several switches/VLANs and four separate FWLB load balancers for complete redundancy. Most vendors that offer an SLB solution also offer FWLB solutions, often with the same equipment as SLB.

The best way to handle site security is to look at the site's throughput and security needs, and to create a solution accordingly. A site's design and administration team is ultimately responsible for the site.

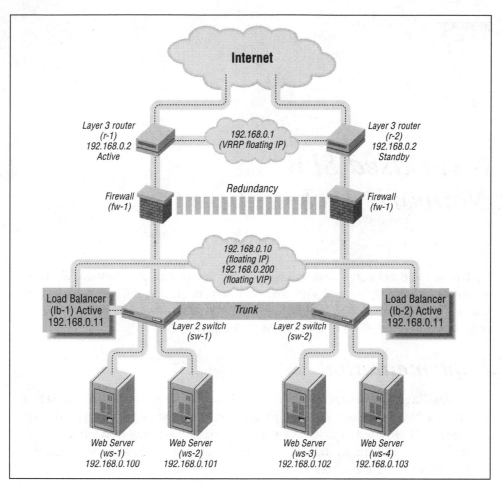

Figure 6-4. Flat-based SLB with a firewall

7

NAT-Based SLB
Network Architecture

NAT-based SLB network architecture is, by definition, any SLB network implementation where the IPs of the VIPs and real servers are on different subnets. It is named NAT because the load balancer NATs packets traveling between two subnets, much like a firewall or a router performing a NAT.

Implementation

The main difference between NAT- and flat-based architectures is that the SLB unit performs a NAT from one network to another. The best and most typical way to implement NAT-based SLB is with a route-path, two-armed configuration. In Figure 7-1, the SLB device translates normal routed IP addresses (represented by the nonrouted 192.168.0.0/24 IP space) into nonrouted IPs, on which the web servers sit.

In this configuration the servers are on a separate VLAN from the VIP addresses on the load balancers. On the public network, the only floating IPs between the active and standby load balancers are the VIP addresses. There is no need for a floating default gateway (such as 192.168.0.10 in the flat-based example) on the public network, since the load balancers aren't acting as default routes on that network. The floating gateway is included on the private network (10.0.0.1 in the following figures). The load balancers can also function as firewalls because they have such tight control over traffic flow.

Sometimes NAT-based SLB is implemented, but, in this method, all devices share one LAN. The load balancers are configured for multiple networks on the same LAN, and they perform the NAT themselves. We see this type of configuration in Figure 7-2.

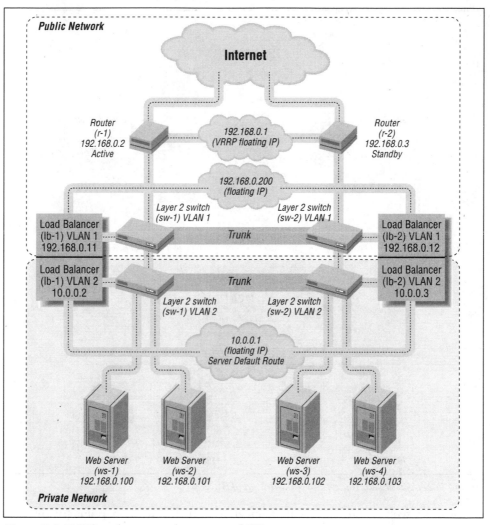

Figure 7-1. NAT-based, route-path, two-armed SLB

The load balancers are configured for two subnets on the same LAN, one for the public interfaces for the VIPs, and another for the web server's private subnet. Even though everything is on the same LAN, the load balancer still performs the NAT.

From both a security and an architectural standpoint, it's better to use a two-armed configuration with two separate LANs (or two VLANs). Putting everything on one LAN defeats several of the security objectives and advantages of a NAT-based configuration. Keeping an actual barrier between the server and public network reinforces the overall security of a site. Traffic flow is easier to manage with two

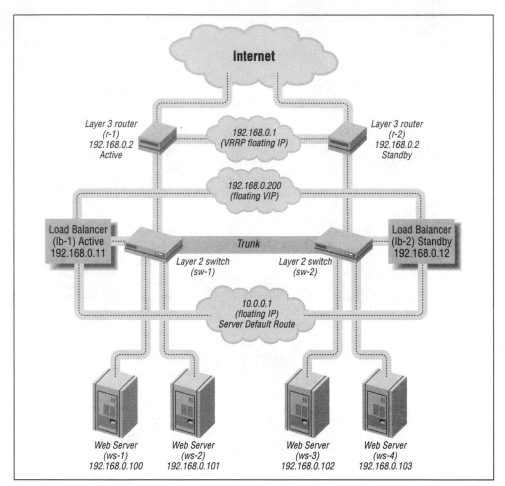

Figure 7-2. NAT-based, route-path, one-armed SLB

(V)LANs as well. There is a clear delineation and demarcation point for the two separate networks, making troubleshooting, in many cases, much easier.

Bridge-Path and DSR

Because NAT from one network to another is a Layer 3 function, bridge-path isn't an option for NAT-based SLB. For NAT to work, the load balancer must have interfaces on two networks, and bridge-path generally involves only one network.

DSR is not as common in a NAT-based scenario as it is in a flat-based setup, but it is possible. Unlike flat-based scenarios, a Layer 3 device is required in addition to the load balancer and Layer 2 infrastructure to work with DSR. As per a DSR scenario, the packets have already been rewritten on the way out of the actual servers with no need for any more processing. The Layer 3 device simply forwards the packets from one network to another—a process that is resource-intensive but saves the load balancer some work. In Figure 7-3, we see an example of a NAT-based configuration with DSR.

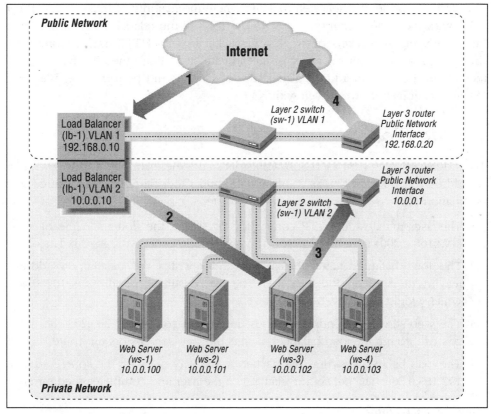

Figure 7-3. NAT-based network topology with DSR

The redundancy component was removed to better show how DSR would fit into this type of scenario. A packet comes to the load balancer (step 1) and is sent to a web server, such as ws-3 (step 2). The web server then sends the packet out already rewritten (step 3), but it still needs to be forwarded to the public network so it can get to the Internet. The Layer 3 device forwards the packet unchanged to the public network and then on to its destination (step 4), without adding any additional load to the load balancer. The actual load on the Layer 3 device is minimal, since all it is doing is forwarding packets with no processing.

Why NAT-Based?

There are several advantages to NAT-based SLB, most of which involve the extra security that a NATed connection can provide, especially when the servers are on a nonrouted RFC 1918 address space. When dealing with servers on a nonrouted IP space, you have a great deal of control over how the servers are actually seen by the world.

This architecture lends itself well to a site where the majority of traffic is HTTP (or SSL). With the added security of the NATed IPs and the relatively low in-out ratio (approximately 10 packets out for every packet in with HTTP traffic, while hundreds of packets go out for every packet in with streaming), the NAT-based architecture can provide an additional measure of security and performance. Web and SSL applications both work well with NAT.

Traffic Flow

To understand how flat-based SLB works, let's take the example of a user with an IP address off 200.200.200.20. Table 7-1 illustrates the changes in IP source and destination addresses. The process takes four steps:

1. The user initiates an HTTP connection by typing the domain name of vip-1 (192.168.0.200) into the browser. The connection goes to the load balancer.

2. The load balancer takes the packet and rewrites the destination address, leaving the source address as it is. The new destination address is 10.0.0.100, which would be the web server ws-1.

3. The web server responds and sends traffic back to 200.200.200.20. The traffic passes through the load balancer, as it is the web server's default route.

4. The load balancer rewrites the packet on the way out with the source address 192.168.0.200. The packet travels back to the user and completes the journey.

Table 7-1. Packet translation

Step	Source IP address	Destination IP address
1	200.200.200.20	192.168.0.200
2	200.200.200.20	10.0.0.100
3	10.0.0.100	200.200.200.20
4	192.168.0.200	200.200.200.20

Network Configuration

The following sections outline some basic IP configurations that may be used as examples for setup and installation of NAT-based SLB networks. The redundancy and wiring are typical for this type of scenario but are by no means the only ways to implement an SLB site. These configuration examples are used in the chapters involving specific vendor configurations.

Routers

The routers are configured exactly as in the flat-based topology (see Table 7-2). Two routers, one active and one standby, are configured with a floating IP address between them. The active unit is given a VRRP priority of 200, while the standby is given 100.

Table 7-2. Router network configuration

Unit	r-1 (active)	r-2 (standby)
IP address	192.168.0.2	192.168.0.3
Subnet mask	255.255.255.0	255.255.255.0
VRRP IP address	192.168.0.1	192.168.0.1
VRRP priority	200	100

SLB Units

The SLB units are configured a bit differently in Table 7-3. The VLAN 1 configuration is identical to the flat-based network architecture, while in the NAT architecture, there is a whole other network configured on VLAN 2. Different products have different ways of denoting which interfaces are outside and which are internal. Switch-based load balancers allow you to set VLANs, while server-based load-balancers usually have those roles labeled in their Ethernet interfaces.

Table 7-3. SLB network configuration

Unit	lb-1 (active)	lb-2 (standby)
IP address (VLAN 1)	192.168.0.11	192.168.0.12
Subnet mask	255.255.255.0	255.255.255.0
Shared address	192.168.0.10	192.168.0.10
Default route	192.168.0.1	192.168.0.1
IP address (VLAN 2)	10.0.0.2	10.0.0.3
Subnet mask	255.255.255.0	255.255.255.0
Shared address	10.0.0.1	10.0.0.1

You may notice a similar numbering and configuration scheme of VLAN 2 to the routers r-1 and r-2. This is because the SLB units are acting as routers and are the default gateways for all web servers. Because of the similar function, it simplifies matters greatly to configure them like the routers.

Again, notice that there is no floating default route between the two load balancers on the public VLAN, while a shared IP is on the private VLAN. Since there are no servers on the public VLAN, there isn't a need for the load balancers to serve as a default route on that network.

Web Servers

In Table 7-4, the web servers are configured on the nonrouted IP address space rather than routable IP address space. Other than that difference, they are configured exactly as with the flat-based network architecture. The default routes are configured to point towards the load balancers.

Table 7-4. Web server network configuration

Unit	ws-1	ws-2	ws-3	ws-4
IP address	10.0.0.100	10.0.0.101	10.0.0.102	10.0.0.103
Subnet mask	255.255.255.0	255.255.255.0	255.255.255.0	255.255.255.0
Default route	10.0.0.1	10.0.0.1	10.0.0.1	10.0.0.1
Service and port	HTTP:80	HTTP:80	HTTP:80	HTTP:80

VIP Configuration

The VIP configuration is shown in Table 7-5. The VIP is, of course, on the routable IP address space, while the real servers are located on the nonrouted IP address space. The SLB units serve to perform the NAT between the two networks.

Table 7-5. VIP configuration

VIP	vip-1
IP address	192.168.0.200
Subnet mask	255.255.255.0
Service and port	HTTP:80
Real servers (active)	10.0.0.100, 10.0.0.101, 10.0.0.102, 10.0.0.103

Individual Pass-Through VIPs

Since the web servers aren't directly available to the Internet, it may be necessary to set up additional VIPs, each corresponding with an individual web server. This would allow a user to browse each individual server, which can be useful for troubleshooting and individual administration. This type of VIP is called an "individual pass-through" (see Table 7-6).

Table 7-6. Pass-through VIP configuration

VIP	vip-1	vip-2	vip-3	vip-4
IP address	192.168.0.100	192.168.0.101	192.168.0.102	192.168.0.103
Subnet mask	255.255.255.0	255.255.255.0	255.255.255.0	255.255.255.0
Real server	10.0.0.100	10.0.0.101	10.0.0.102	10.0.0.103
Service and port	HTTP:80	HTTP:80	HTTP:80	HTTP:80

Switches

There are two ways to implement switches into a NAT-based scenario: using separate switches for the public network and server networks or using the same switches with VLAN separation. Which is more appropriate primarily depends on budgetary and security concerns.

One way to implement switches is to take a switch (or pair of switches) and divide it into two separate VLANs. By electronically separating the LANs, the traffic for each network is sequestered. Implementing VLANs often provides cost saving in equipment, additional flexibility in port configuration, and easier management, all while still offering a measure of security. Another way to implement switches is to use separate switches for the public LANs and the private server LAN. Some smaller switches do not offer the VLAN feature. If a site is using hubs rather than switches, there can be separate hubs for the public network and the private server network.

Some security experts are wary of having a single device separating two LANs electronically. They would prefer to have the two networks separated physically. If everything is protected by a firewall, this shouldn't be much of an issue. Again, it's up to each site's administrator to decide. In any case, the public network traffic should be separated in some manner from the private server network for security and troubleshooting reasons. Also, it just makes for a neater, cleaner network.

IEEE 802.1Q VLAN tagging

When connecting two switches with one single LAN (such as the flat-network architecture), you only need a crossover cable. However, when implementing multiple VLANs on a set of switches, it becomes more beneficial to employ something called IEEE 802.1Q VLAN tagging. Also known as VLAN tagging, this protocol allows you to connect more than one VLAN over a single trunk between switches. VLAN tagging does this by adding a few bytes to the Ethernet frame, which denotes the VLAN from which the frame originated. Cisco has a proprietary implementation of 802.1Q tagging known as Inter-Switch Link (ISL), which operates in essentially the same manner.

Several thousand VLANs can communicate over one link (assuming the bandwidth of the VLANs does not exceed the link). It is a good idea to use a GigE port for this purpose, although other port speeds will work. It is simply a matter of how much traffic you have running between the two switches and on which VLAN the traffic flows. In several of the NAT-based SLB examples, an 802.1Q VLAN trunk is used between sw-1 and sw-2. This allows us to use one interconnect for VLAN 1 and VLAN 2, simplifying the configuration.

Redundancy

Because of the routing nature of NAT-based configurations, redundancy is done on Layer 3, usually with some type of VRRP or similar setup. Fail-over time is nearly instantaneous in most cases. VRRP with load balancers involves a shared IP address between two devices with only one of the devices actually using the IP. When dealing with two subnets, it's important to make sure that the active unit is active for both subnets. In most situations, traffic must go out on the same load balancer from which it came. If one load balancer is master for the VIPs, and the other is master for default route IP for the servers, then SLB will not work.

In Figure 7-4, we see a situation where both the public and private networks have floating IP's on the same load balancer, lb-1. This is critical to SLB operation.

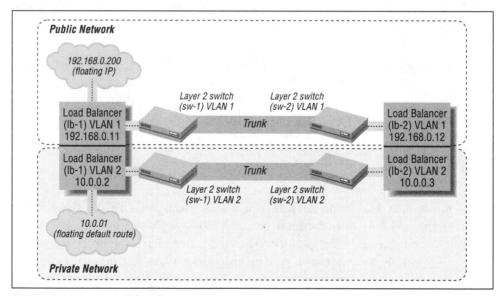

Figure 7-4. A correct redundancy scenario

In Figure 7-5, we see where the public network has its floating IP on lb-1, and the private server network's floating IP is active on lb-2. The traffic will go in lb-1 and try to go back out through lb-2, but since it has none of the real-time TCP sequence information or stateful information from lb-1, SLB will not work.

Security

Perhaps the greatest advantage to this type of infrastructure is security. While not recommended as a total security solution, the SLB unit can double as a firewall by allowing only traffic that is destined for the desired services. In addition, with this type of network, the web servers have no direct contact with the Internet, which

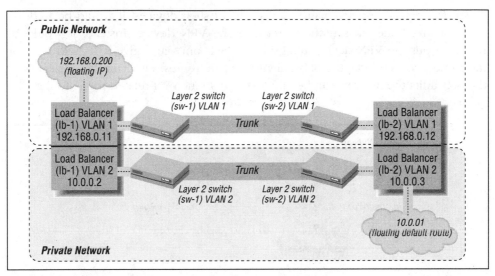

Figure 7-5. An incorrect redundancy scenario

increases their security. While it's always better to have a device built for security (such as a firewall) protecting a site, sometimes one isn't available due to budget constraints. This is a case where a load balancer with a NAT based configuration can add a level of security not otherwise available.

The most common uses of firewalls in a web-serving scenario are packet filtering and stateful inspection. Packet filtering blocks traffic through IPs and ports, and stateful inspection keeps track of related TCP-connections and various rules. By their very nature, most SLB devices only allow traffic to proceed to certain IPs and ports on the network, such as port 80 on the web servers, and are mindful of state. Traffic proceeds to specific ports and VIPs, not to individual web servers (unless this is a requirement, and even then it is not direct). Unless there is a specific need for other firewall functions, such as VPN or packet-inspection (which is unwise at high traffic levels, since it is very likely the firewall would not be able to handle the traffic), then the SLB device could (I stress could) serve as a firewall.

Only those responsible for a site are qualified to make security decisions. Load balancers aren't built specifically for security, but many load balancers do offer security features. Even when used in conjunction with a firewall, they can offer additional security measures.

VPN

It is sometimes necessary to put a Virtual Private Network (VPN) in place for administration purposes. A VPN creates a virtual tunnel for packets to traverse over a public network. This tunnel is most often encrypted for additional security.

Given the probable performance limitations of such devices, it would be undesirable for all of the site's traffic to traverse the VPN device. Instead, it would be better to put the VPN device alongside the SLB units and give it IP addresses on the same two networks the SLB units use. Static routes, either in the servers or in the SLB units themselves, can be employed to shunt VPN-related traffic to the VPN devices. Such a scenario is seen in Figure 7-6.

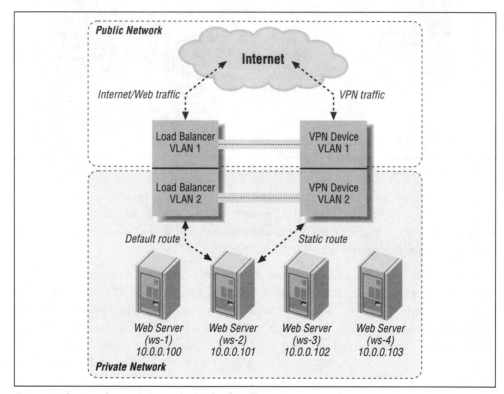

Figure 7-6. VPN devices not in the path of traffic

III

Configuring Server Load Balancers

8

Alteon WebSystems

Alteon is the maker of Layer 2–7 switches and is a part of Nortel Networks. The line of switches being produced by Alteon is still under the Alteon brand and includes the ACEDirector and 180 series of switches, which run the Alteon WebOS code.

The ACEDirector series of switches includes 10/100 switches, usually with eight Fast Ethernet and one Gigabit Ethernet port, while the 180 series offers expanded performance and up to 9 ports that can be either Fast Ethernet (Cat 5 copper) or Gigabit Ethernet (SX fiber). They are pizza-box-style stackable switches with a chassis series available, but at the time of this writing, the 700 series chassis switches do not support the code reviewed in this chapter. Check with an Alteon sales representative or the web site for more detailed information. This product's specifications are:

> Vendor: Alteon WebSystems
> Model: ACEswitch 184
> Software Revision: WebOS 8.0.43
> Platform: Switch
> Ports: 9x, 10/100/1000, Fast Ethernet/Gigabit Ethernet ports

The Alteon series of load balancers can be put in a wide variety of configurations and is one of the most flexible products on the market. It supports flat-based in route-path, bridge-path, and DSR configurations, as well as NAT-based in one-armed and two-armed configurations. This chapter discusses the flat-based, route-path, one-armed architecture, as well as the NAT-based, route-path, two-armed architecture. However, Alteon can support a number of other configurations.

Introduction to the CLI

The Command-Line Interface (CLI) for Alteon's WebOS is very different from the other switch-based products presented in this book. The other products closely follow the look, feel, and command sets of Cisco's IOS, while Alteon's WebOS takes a different approach, based more on directory structure. The initial menu to the superuser account looks like this:

```
----------------------------------------------------------------
[Main Menu]
       info   - Information Menu
       stats  - Statistics Menu
       cfg    - Configuration Menu
       oper   - Operations Command Menu
       boot   - Boot Options Menu
       maint  - Maintenance Menu
       diff   - Show pending config changes   [global command]
       apply  - Apply pending config changes [global command]
       save   - Save updated config to FLASH [global command]
       revert - Revert pending or applied changes [global command]
       exit   - Exit  [global command, always available]

>> Main#
```

Commands are typed in almost the same manner as the directory tree in DOS or Unix. For example, if you want to show the current boot configuration, you can go into the */boot* subdirectory:

```
>> Main# /boot
----------------------------------------------------------------
[Boot Options Menu]
       image  - Select software image to use on next boot
       conf   - Select config block to use on next boot
       tftp   - Download new software image via TFTP
       reset  - Reset switch [WARNING: Restarts Spanning Tree]
       cur    - Display current boot options
```

Then you would issue the *cur* command:

```
>> Boot Options# cur
Currently set to boot software image1, active config block.
Current FLASH software:
  image1: version 8.0.30
  image2: empty
  maintenance kernel: version 8.0.30

>> Boot Options#
```

You can also invoke a command by including its full pathname, no matter where you are in the command directory structure:

```
>> Main# /boot/cur
Currently set to boot software image2, active config block.
Current FLASH software:
```

```
      image1: version 8.0.30
      image2: version 8.0.43, downloaded  3:02:25 Fri Sep 22, 2000
      maintenance kernel: version 8.0.30
```

```
   >> Boot Options#
```

When the command is executed, it will drop you into the directory of that command. For instance, even though you were in the root directory, /, after the command */boot/conf* was executed, you were dropped into the */boot* directory.

An important thing to remember with Alteon's WebOS is that for any changes to take effect, you need to run the *apply* command:

```
   >> Main# apply
   -------------------------------------------------------------------
   Apply complete; don't forget to "save" updated configuration.
   .

   >> Main#
```

For the configuration to be effective on the next boot, you also need to run the *save* command to save the changes to the flash RAM:

```
   >> Main# save

   Request will first copy the FLASH "active" config to "backup",
    then overlay FLASH "active" with new config.
   Confirm saving to FLASH [y/n]: y
   New config successfully saved to FLASH.

   >> Main#
```

Commands that have arguments can be done one of two ways. You can either issue the command and be prompted for an argument, as in the real server naming command:

```
   >> Real server 1 # name

   Enter new real server name: ws-1
```

or you can specify the argument after the command, skipping the prompt:

```
   >> Real server 1 # name ws-1
   Current real server name:
   New real server name:     ws-1
```

There are many other nuances to WebOS that are not explored in this chapter. Practice and Alteon manuals will help to familiarize oneself with the CLI. There is also a web-based interface, but I won't delve into that in this book.

Getting Started

Fresh off the factory line, the Alteon unit will act as a Layer 2 switch without any configuration. To start the configuration, find the appropriate cable (there is a DB-9 male to DB-9 female straight, non-null modem cable usually included) to plug into the DB-9 male port. Hit Enter and you should get a password prompt such as this:

```
Enter password:
```

The default password is *admin*. Once logged in, you should see this:

```
Enter password:
System Information at  3:42:41 Fri Jul 14, 2000

ACEswitch 184
sysName:
sysLocation:
Last boot:  2:56:02 Fri Jul 14, 2000 (power cycle)

MAC address: 00:60:cf:45:8e:a0    IP (If 1) address: 0.0.0.0
Hardware Revision: B
Hardware Part No: C05_5A-D_6A-D
Software Version 8.0.43 (FLASH image1), factory default configuration.


The switch is booted with factory default configuration.
  To ease the configuration of the switch, a "Set Up" facility which
  will prompt you with those configuration items that are essential
  to the operation of the switch is provided.
Would you like to run "Set Up" to configure the switch? [y/n]
```

When booted for the first time, the unit prompts you to run its default configuration script. Select **n** to that. If there is ever a need to execute this script at another time, it can be run by entering the command, */cfg/setup*.

The first step is to set up the network. To do this, go into the */cfg/ip* menu to configure the IP options:

```
>> Main# /cfg/ip
------------------------------------------------------------
[IP Menu]
      if      - Interface Menu
      gw      - Default Gateway Menu
      route   - Static Route Menu
      frwd    - Forwarding Menu
      rip1    - Routing Information Protocol menu
      bgp     - Border Gateway Protocol menu
      port    - IP Port Menu
      dns     - Domain Name System Menu
      log     - Set IP address of syslog host
      log2    - Set IP address of second syslog host
      logfac  - Set facility of syslog host
      log2fac - Set facility of second syslog host
```

```
        rearp   - Set re-ARP period in minutes
        metrc   - Set default gateway metric
        cur     - Display current IP configuration

  >> IP#
```

You want the `if` menu to configure the IP interfaces on the device. The Alteon allows up to 256 configured IP interfaces, but you will configure only one interface. If the NAT-based SLB method is employed, then an additional interface will be configured:

```
> IP# if
Enter interface number: (1-256) 1
------------------------------------------------------------
[IP Interface 1 Menu]
        addr    - Set IP address
        mask    - Set subnet mask
        broad   - Set broadcast address
        vlan    - Set VLAN number
        ena     - Enable IP interface
        dis     - Disable IP interface
        del     - Delete IP interface
        cur     - Display current interface configuration

  >> IP Interface 1#
```

The menu is fairly straightforward; you'll need to give the basic IP information and enable the interface:

```
>> IP Interface 1# addr 129.168.0.10
Current IP address:             0.0.0.0
New pending IP address:         192.168.0.10
Pending new subnet mask:        255.255.255.0
Pending new broadcast address:  192.168.0.255
```

If the switch is freshly configured, BOOTP will be enabled by default. By assigning and IP address, you'll be prompted to disable BOOTP. You'll want to select `y` to that:

```
Switch is set to use BOOTP for IP address assignment.
Do you want to DISABLE the use of BOOTP? [y/n] y
Use of BOOTP disabled.
```

Ensure that the subnet mask and broadcast addresses are correct for your IP environment:

```
>> IP Interface 1# mask 255.255.255.0
Current subnet mask:     0.0.0.0
New pending subnet mask: 255.255.255.0

>> IP Interface 1# broad 192.168.0.255
Current broadcast address:     255.255.255.255
New pending broadcast address: 192.168.0.255
```

You must also enable the interface to make the IP address active:

```
>> IP Interface 1# ena
Current status: disabled
New status:     enabled

>> IP Interface 1#
```

By default, new interfaces are set on VLAN 1. If you are using multiple subnets on one LAN, you can assign multiple interfaces to a single VLAN. If the NAT-based SLB method is employed, an interface will be configured on VLAN 2.

You must also configure the default route. This configuration is in the */cfg/ip* menu under **gw**:

```
>> IP# gw
Enter default gateway number: (1-4) 1
-------------------------------------------------------------
[Default gateway 1 Menu]
      addr    - Set IP address
      intr    - Set interval between ping attempts
      retry   - Set number of failed attempts to declare gateway DOWN
      arp     - Enable/disable ARP only health checks
      ena     - Enable default gateway
      dis     - Disable default gateway
      del     - Delete default gateway
      cur     - Display current default gateway configuration

>> Default gateway 1#
```

The Alteon's WebOS allows you to configure more than one gateway, but you only need one. Give the IP address of the default gateway with the *addr* command:

```
>> Default gateway 1# addr 10.24.0.1
Current IP address:     0.0.0.0
New pending IP address: 10.24.0.1
```

and enable the gateway:

```
>> Default gateway 1# ena
Current status: disabled
New status:     enabled

>> Default gateway 1#
```

For SLB to work, you must also enable Layer 4 functions. To do so, go into the */cfg/slb* menu:

```
>> Main# /cfg/slb
-------------------------------------------------------------
[Layer 4 Menu]
      real    - Real Server Menu
      group   - Real Server Group Menu
      virt    - Virtual Server Menu
      filt    - Filtering Menu
```

```
port      - Layer 4 Port Menu
gslb      - Global SLB Menu
url       - URL Resource Definition Menu
sync      - Config Synch Menu
adv       - Layer 4 Advanced Menu
on        - Globally turn Layer 4 processing ON
off       - Globally turn Layer 4 processing OFF
cur       - Display current Layer 4 configuration

>> Layer 4#
```

Simply use the *on* command to enable SLB:

```
>> Layer 4# on
Current status: OFF
New status:     ON
```

Remember, for all these changes to take effect, you must issue an *apply* command, as well as a *save* command, for the configuration to be active upon rebooting. If the switch is fresh, then BOOTP can be disabled completely only with a reboot:

```
> Layer 4# apply
-----------------------------------------------------------------
Apply complete; don't forget to "save" updated configuration.
Also note that the following changes are still pending,
 waiting for a reset of the switch to take effect:
Current value...   new value...
------------------------------
Use of BOOTP enabled => disabled

>> Layer 4# save
Request will first copy the FLASH "active" config to "backup",
 then overlay FLASH "active" with new config.
Confirm saving to FLASH [y/n]: y
New config successfully saved to FLASH.
```

Now would be a good time to reset the switch (make sure you have performed a *save*) with the */boot/reset* command. This is required to disable BOOTP if the switch is freshly configured and is also a good way to test your network settings.

```
>> Main# /boot/reset
Reset will use software "image2" and the active config block.
>> Note that this will RESTART the Spanning Tree,
>> which will likely cause an interruption in network service.
Confirm reset [y/n]: y
Resetting at 14:35:51 Sat Sep 30, 2000...
```

Security

The first security measure is achieved by getting rid of the default password, *admin*. From the main menu, select the user administration menu with the command */cfg/sys/user*:

```
>> Main# /cfg/sys/user
---------------------------------------------------------------
[User Access Control Menu]
      usrpw   - Set user password (user)
      sopw    - Set SLB operator password (slboper)
      l4opw   - Set L4 operator password (l4oper)
      opw     - Set operator password (oper)
      sapw    - Set SLB administrator password (slbadmin)
      l4apw   - Set L4 administrator password (l4admin)
      admpw   - Set administrator password (admin)
      cur     - Display current user status

>> User Access Control#
```

 Be sure to use good security practices when setting passwords. Use nondictionary words and combine letters and numbers. Also, be sure to change passwords only over the serial console or SSH, or on a secure LAN connection, to prevent the password from being sniffed.

The default wouldn't be hard to guess, so it is critical that it is changed. The command *admpw* allows you to change the *admin* password:

```
>> User Access Control# admpw
Changing ADMINISTRATOR password; validation required...
Enter current administrator password:
Enter new administrator password:
Re-enter new administrator password:
New administrator password accepted.
```

As always with WebOS, *cur* shows the current configuration for the options located in a particular submenu:

```
Usernames:
  user      - Enabled
  slboper   - Disabled
  l4oper    - Disabled
  oper      - Disabled
  slbadmin  - Disabled
  l4admin   - Disabled
  admin     - Always Enabled


>> User Access Control#
```

WebOS provides several possible levels of security that can be useful in different circumstances. Only the **user** and **admin** accounts are enabled by default, however. The **user** account gives read-only access into the system, which is good for getting information such as statistics and the statuses of the various services. The menu for the **user** account is much more limited:

```
        -----------------------------------------------------------
        [Main Menu]
              info    - Information Menu
              stats   - Statistics Menu
              exit    - Exit  [global command, always available]

        >> Main>
```

 WebOS does not prompt you for a username, only a password. (This is true even with SSH access.) The password you give will determine which account you log into. Because of this, every account's password must be unique.

The default password for the user account is **user**, so this should also be changed using the command *usrpw*. You will be asked for the *admin* password to change the **user** account password:

```
        >> User Access Control# usrpw
        Changing USER password; validation required...
        Enter current administrator password:
        Enter new user password:
        Re-enter new user password:
        New user password accepted.

        >> User Access Control#
```

To enable an account, simply supply it with a password. Inversely, to disable an account, make the password null, which automatically disables the account.

Encrypted Access

As of Version 8.0 and later, the AD4 and 184 models of Alteon Web switches provide the means to employ SSH for command-line administration. Earlier models such as the AD3 and 180E do not have SSH capabilities because they do not have sufficient memory to hold SSH capabilities in flash. Configuration of SSH can be done only at the console serial port. To enable SSH, go into the SSHD configuration menu in */cfg/sys/sshd*:

```
        >> Main# /cfg/sys/sshd
        -----------------------------------------------------------
        [SSHD Menu]
              intrval - Set Interval for generating the RSA server key
              scpadm  - Set SCP-only admin password
              hkeygen - Generate the RSA host key
              skeygen - Generate the RSA server key
              ena     - Enable the SCP apply and save
              dis     - Disable the SCP apply and save
```

```
       on      - Turn SSH server ON
       off     - Turn SSH server OFF
       cur     - Display current SSH server configuration

>> SSHD# on
Current status: OFF
New status:    ON
```

Execute the *apply* command, and all of the necessary keys will be generated:

```
>> SSHD# apply

RSA host key generation starts ..............................................
RSA host key generation completes (lasts 113898 ms)
RSA host key is being saved to Flash ROM, please don't reboot
the box immediately.

RSA server key generation starts ............................................
RSA server key generation completes (lasts 66692 ms)
RSA server key is being saved to Flash ROM, please don't reboot
the box immediately.
------------------------------------------------------------------
Apply complete; don't forget to "save" updated configuration.

>> SSHD# cur
RSA server key autogen disabled
SCP-only administrator password configured
RSA host key currently ready to service
RSA server key currently ready to service
SCP apply and save currently enabled
SSH server currently ON
```

WebOS also allows you to use SCP to transfer configuration files. Check the Alteon documentation for details.

Flat-Based SLB

Following the blueprint from Chapter 6, you will now configure the Alteon Web switch pair (see Table 8-1). This will be a flat-based, route-path, one-armed configuration. Thus far, lb-1 has been given the IP address of 192.168.0.11 and lb-2 has been given 192.168.0.12.

Table 8-1. Load balancer IP configuration

Unit	lb-1 (active)	lb-2 (standby)
IP address	192.168.0.11	192.168.0.12
Subnet mask	255.255.255.0	255.255.255.0
Shared address	192.168.0.10	192.168.0.10
Default route	192.168.0.1	192.168.0.1

The subnet masks and default routes should already have been configured. Configure the web servers to their respective IP addresses as specified in the flat-network architecture shown in Table 8-2.

Table 8-2. Web server IP configuration

Unit	ws-1	ws-2	ws-3	ws-4
IP address	192.168.0.100	192.168.0.101	192.168.0.102	192.168.0.103
Subnet mask	255.255.255.0	255.255.255.0	255.255.255.0	255.255.255.0
Default route	192.168.0.10	192.168.0.10	192.168.0.10	192.168.0.10
Service and port	HTTP:80	HTTP:80	HTTP:80	HTTP:80

With the servers and load balancers configured, we can begin configuring the load-balancing portion of the Alteon. The SLB portion of the Alteon configuration is found at */cfg/slb*:

```
>> Real server 1 # /cfg/slb
-------------------------------------------------------------

[Layer 4 Menu]
        real    - Real Server Menu
        group   - Real Server Group Menu
        virt    - Virtual Server Menu
        filt    - Filtering Menu
        port    - Layer 4 Port Menu
        gslb    - Global SLB Menu
        url     - URL Resource Definition Menu
        sync    - Config Synch Menu
        adv     - Layer 4 Advanced Menu
        on      - Globally turn Layer 4 processing ON
        off     - Globally turn Layer 4 processing OFF
        cur     - Display current Layer 4 configuration

>> Layer 4#
```

Ports

With Alteon, you must first configure the ports involved to handle SLB traffic. This is critical because, if this is not configured, SLB will not work. This is under the *port* submenu:

```
>> Layer 4# port
Enter port number: (1-9) 1
-------------------------------------------------------------

[SLB port 1 Menu]
        client  - Enable/disable client processing
        server  - Enable/disable server processing
        hotstan - Enable/disable hot-standby processing
        intersw - Enable/disable inter-switch processing
        proxy   - Enable/disable use of PIP for ingress traffic
        pip     - Set Proxy IP address for port
```

```
filt    - Enable/disable filtering
add     - Add filter to port
rem     - Remove filter from port
cur     - Display current port configuration
```

There are two types of processing that each port can do: client processing and server processing. Client processing is the half of the connection on the client's or user's side. Server processing is the part of the connection that takes place on the server side. Since this is the flat-based network architecture, the port will be handling both:

```
>> SLB port 1# client
Current client processing: disabled
Enter new client processing [d/e]: e

>> SLB port 1# server
Current server processing: disabled
Enter new server processing [d/e]: e
```

Real Servers

Under the */cfg/slb/* directory, select **rea** . You will be asked which real server you want to configure. The Alteons have a finite number of real servers you can configure with a limit of 255 on the model used here (the Alteon ACEDirector 184). For ws-1, we'll select 1:

```
>> Layer 4# real
Enter real server number: (1-255) 1
-------------------------------------------------------------
[Real server 1  Menu]
     rip     - Set IP addr of real server
     name    - Set server name
     weight  - Set server weight
     maxcon  - Set maximum number of connections
     tmout   - Set minutes inactive connection remains open
     backup  - Set backup real server
     inter   - Set interval between health checks
     retry   - Set number of failed attempts to declare server DOWN
     restr   - Set number of successful attempts to declare server UP
     addlb   - Add URL path for URL load balance
     remlb   - Remove URL path for URL load balance
     remote  - Enable/disable remote site operation
     proxy   - Enable/disable client proxy operation
     submac  - Enable/disable source MAC address substitution
     nocook  - Enable/disable no available URL cookie operation
     exclude - Enable/disable exclusionary string matching
     ena     - Enable real server
     dis     - Disable real server
     del     - Delete real server
     cur     - Display current real server configuration

>> Real server 1 #
```

First, you'll configure the `rip`, the real IP address with 192.168.0.100:

```
>> Real server 1 # rip
Current real server IP address: 0.0.0.0
Enter new real server IP address: 192.168.0.100
```

For the flat-based SLB with the Alteon as your default route (Layer 3 path), you must enable `submac` for every real server:

```
>> Real server 1 # submac
Current source MAC substitution: disabled
Enter new source MAC substitution [d/e]: e
```

 If you fail to enable `submac` for a real server and you are using the Alteon as the default route for your servers (as opposed to the Layer 2 path), it will most likely cause serious problems on your network.

You'll also need to set the `name`, just to keep things neat:

```
>> Real server 1 # name
Current real server name:
Enter new real server name: ws-1
```

There are other options you can set for this real server, depending on your individual needs, such as concepts. Check the documentation to see what applies to your particular situation.

Apply and save the changes, then check the status with the command */info/slb/ real 1*:

```
>> Real server 1 # /info/slb/real 1
  1: ws-1, 08:00:20:d9:63:2c, vlan 1, port 1, health 3, up

>> Server Load Balancing Information#
```

This shows that real server 1, named ws-1, reporting a MAC address of 08:00:20: d9:63:2c, is on VLAN 1, connected through port 1, and is registering as up. Follow those steps for ws-2 through ws-4. When done, apply and save the configuration.

Groups

Alteon's WebOS, like some other vendors, has an extra abstraction layer between the real servers and the VIPs. This is known as a group, and it offers some additional flexibility in the configurations. Groups in Alteon's WebOS allow special health-checking configurations, the ability to set up a backup real server or group in case the primary group fails, as well as some other features that give added flexibility for SLB.

There are also a limited number of groups available; 256 are on the model used in this config. We will configure group 1, which will later be associated with vip-1:

```
>> Layer 4# /cfg/slb/group 1
--------------------------------------------------------------
[Real server group 1 Menu]
      metric  - Set metric used to select next server in group
      content - Set health check content
      health  - Set health check type
      backup  - Set backup real server or group
      name    - Set real server group name
      realthr - Set real server failure threshold
      add     - Add real server
      rem     - Remove real server
      del     - Delete real server group
      cur     - Display current group configuration

>> Real server group 1#
```

Add the real servers to this group with the *add* command:

```
>> Real server group 1# add
Enter real server number: (1-255) 1
```

Give it the name of **group-1** with the *name* command:

```
>> Real server group 1# name
Current real server group name:
Enter new real server group name: group-1
```

Apply and save your changes.

VIPs

Alteon refers to VIPs as Virtual Servers. The nomenclature is different, but the concept is the same. This is where you will point all of the user traffic. The VIP menu is under */cfg/slb*, as *virt*. As with the real servers and groups, there is a limited number available in Alteon's WebOS, which is 256 on the model used here:

```
>> Layer 4# virt 1
--------------------------------------------------------------
[Virtual Server 1 Menu]
      service - Virtual Service Menu
      vip     - Set IP addr of virtual server
      dname   - Set domain name of virtual server
      cont    - Set BW Contract
      layr3   - Enable/disable layer 3 only balancing
      ftpp    - Enable/disable FTP SLB parsing for virtual server
      ena     - Enable virtual server
      dis     - Disable virtual server
      del     - Delete virtual server
      cur     - Display current virtual configuration

>> Virtual Server 1#
```

To configure the IP address of the VIP, use the *vip* command:

```
>> Virtual Server 1# vip
Current virtual server IP address: 0.0.0.0
Enter new virtual server IP address: 192.168.0.200
```

You also need to enable this virtual server:

```
>> Virtual Server 1# enable
Current status: disabled
New status:     enabled

>> Virtual Server 1#
```

With Alteon's WebOS, we need to enable one service at a time, based on the TCP/UDP port required. There is a submenu called *service*. You will configure port 80 since you are setting this up for web service:

```
>> Virtual Server 1# service/
Enter virtual port: 80
---------------------------------------------------------------
[Virtual Server 1 http Service Menu]
     group    - Set real server group number
     rport    - Set real port
     hname    - Set hostname
     httpslb - Set HTTP SLB processing
     cont     - Set BW contract for this virtual service
     pbind    - Set persistent binding type
     udp      - Enable/disable UDP balancing
     frag     - Enable/disable remapping UDP server fragments
     nonat    - Enable/disable only substituting MAC addresses
     del      - Delete virtual service
     cur      - Display current virtual service configuration

>> Virtual Server 1 http Service#
```

Now, you can bind group 1, which contains real servers ws-1 through ws-4, to this service:

```
>> Virtual Server 1 http Service# group 1
Current real server group:
New pending real server group: 1

>> Virtual Server 1 http Service#
```

You can check the status of the virtual server with the *cur* command:

```
>> Virtual Server 1# cur
Current virtual server 1:
  192.168.0.200, enabled, ftpp disabled
    virtual ports:
      http: rport http, group 1, frags
        real servers:
            1: 192.168.0.100,   weight 1,  enabled, backup none
            2: 192.168.0.101,   weight 1,  enabled, backup none
```

```
      3: 192.168.0.102,    weight 1,   enabled, backup none
      4: 192.168.0.103,    weight 1,   enabled, backup none
```

Apply and save the changes, and the VIP is configured. Point your browser to 192. 168.0.200 and you should get the load-balanced instance.

NAT-Based SLB

With the flat-based architecture, we used only port 1 of the Alteon switch. With the NAT-based architecture, we will also use port 2. This will be a NAT-based, route-path, two-armed configuration (see Table 8-3). Port 1 will be on VLAN 1, just as with the flat-based architecture, and will have the same 192.168.0.0/24 IP addresses. Port 2 will be located on VLAN 2 with the 10.0.0.0/24 IP addresses.

Table 8-3. Load balancer IP configuration

Unit	lb-1 (active)	lb-2 (standby)
IP address (VLAN 1)	192.168.0.11	192.168.0.12
Subnet mask	255.255.255.0	255.255.255.0
Shared address	192.168.0.10	192.168.0.10
Default route	192.168.0.1	192.168.0.1
IP address (VLAN 2)	10.0.0.2	10.0.0.3
Subnet mask	255.255.255.0	255.255.255.0
Shared address	10.0.0.1	10.0.0.1

You've already configured port 1 in the initial setup, but you need to enable client-side processing. As with the flat-based architecture, the ports involved need to be enabled with client- or server-side processing, or both. The client traffic comes in on port 1, so it is client-enabled, and the server traffic is on port 2, thus enabling it for server processing:

```
>> SLB port 1# cur
Current port 1:
    client disabled, server disabled, hotstan disabled, intersw disabled
    proxy disabled, 0.0.0.0
    filt disabled, filters: empty
```

You see that port 1 (*/cfg/slb/port 1/cur*) shows client and server disabled. Enable client (users from the Internet) processing:

```
>> SLB port 1# client
Current client processing: disabled
Enter new client processing [d/e]: e

>> SLB port 1#
```

Do this same procedure with port 2 (*/cfg/slb/port 2/cur*), but instead, enable server processing:

```
>> SLB port 1# server
Current server processing: disabled
Enter new server processing [d/e]: e

>> SLB port 1#
```

The IP address for VLAN 1 was already configured in the setup script as *interface 1*, but now you need to configure VLAN 2 and the appropriate IP address. The command */cfg/sys/if 2* will bring you to the *interface 2* menu:

```
>> SLB port 1# /cfg/ip/if 2
------------------------------------------------------------
[IP Interface 2 Menu]
      addr    - Set IP address
      mask    - Set subnet mask
      broad   - Set broadcast address
      vlan    - Set VLAN number
      ena     - Enable IP interface
      dis     - Disable IP interface
      del     - Delete IP interface
      cur     - Display current interface configuration

>> IP Interface 2#
```

Use the *addr*, *mask*, and *broad* commands to set the IP address, subnet mask, and broadcast addresses:

```
>> IP Interface 2# addr
Current IP address:               0.0.0.0
Enter new IP address:             10.0.0.2
Pending new subnet mask:          255.0.0.0
Pending new broadcast address:    10.255.255.255

>> IP Interface 2# mask
Current subnet mask:      0.0.0.0
Pending new subnet mask:  255.0.0.0
Enter new subnet mask:    255.255.255.0

>> IP Interface 2# broad
Current broadcast address:       255.255.255.255
Pending new broadcast address:   10.255.255.255
Enter new broadcast address:     10.0.0.255

>> IP Interface 2#
```

Assign this interface to a VLAN with the *vlan* command:

```
>> IP Interface 2# vlan
Current VLAN: 1
Enter new VLAN [1-4094]: 2

>> IP Interface 2#
```

Finally, enable the new interface:

```
>> IP Interface 2# ena
Current status: disabled
New status:    enabled

>> IP Interface 2#
```

Apply and save the new configuration. Then go to lb-2 and repeat the process, making adjustments for the IPs assigned to that unit.

Real Servers

Each individual web server will be in the nonrouted IP space, which is 10.0.0.0/24 for the example configurations shown in Table 8-4.

Table 8-4. Web server IP configuration

Unit	ws-1	ws-2	ws-3	ws-4
IP address	10.0.0.100	10.0.0.101	10.0.0.102	10.0.0.103
Subnet mask	255.255.255.0	255.255.255.0	255.255.255.0	255.255.255.0
Default route	10.0.0.1	10.0.0.1	10.0.0.1	10.0.0.1
Service and port	HTTP:80	HTTP:80	HTTP:80	HTTP:80

Under the */cfg/slb/* directory, select **rea** . You will be asked which real server you want to configure. The Alteons have a finite number of real servers you can configure with a limit of 255 on the model used here (for the Alteon ACEDirector it's 184). For ws-1, we'll select 1:

```
>> Layer 4# real
Enter real server number: (1-255) 1
-------------------------------------------------------------
[Real server 1  Menu]
       rip    - Set IP addr of real server
       name   - Set server name
       weight - Set server weight
       maxcon - Set maximum number of connections
       tmout  - Set minutes inactive connection remains open
       backup - Set backup real server
       inter  - Set interval between health checks
       retry  - Set number of failed attempts to declare server DOWN
       restr  - Set number of successful attempts to declare server UP
       addlb  - Add URL path for URL load balance
       remlb  - Remove URL path for URL load balance
       remote - Enable/disable remote site operation
       proxy  - Enable/disable client proxy operation
       submac - Enable/disable source MAC address substitution
       nocook - Enable/disable no available URL cookie operation
       exclude - Enable/disable exclusionary string matching
```

```
     ena     - Enable real server
     dis     - Disable real server
     del     - Delete real server
     cur     - Display current real server configuration

>> Real server 1 #
```

First, configure the **rip**, the real IP address with 10.0.0.100:

```
>> Real server 1 # rip
Current real server IP address: 0.0.0.0
Enter new real server IP address: 10.0.0.100
```

Next, set the **name**, just to keep things neat:

```
>> Real server 1 # name
Current real server name:
Enter new real server name: ws-1
```

There are other options you can set for this real server, depending on your individual needs, such as concepts. Check the documentation to see what applies to your particular situation.

Apply and save the changes, and then check the status with the command */info/ slb/real 1*:

```
>> Real server 1 # /info/slb/real 1
   1: ws-1, 08:00:20:d9:63:2c, vlan 1, port 1, health 3, up

>> Server Load Balancing Information#
```

This shows that real server 1 (ws-1), reporting a MAC address of 08:00:20:d9:63:2c, is on VLAN 1, connected through port 2, and is registering as **up**. Follow the same steps for ws-2 through ws-4. When done, apply and save the config.

Groups

Alteon's WebOS, like some of the other products, has an extra abstraction layer between the real servers and the VIPs. This is known as a group, and it offers some additional flexibility in the configurations. There are also a limited number of groups available, 256 on the model used in this config. You will configure Group 1, which will later be associated with vip-1:

```
>> Layer 4# /cfg/slb/group 1
------------------------------------------------------------
[Real server group 1 Menu]
     metric  - Set metric used to select next server in group
     content - Set health check content
     health  - Set health check type
     backup  - Set backup real server or group
     name    - Set real server group name
     realthr - Set real server failure threshold
```

```
add      - Add real server
rem      - Remove real server
del      - Delete real server group
cur      - Display current group configuration
```

```
>> Real server group 1#
```

Add the real servers to this group with the *add* command:

```
>> Real server group 1# add
Enter real server number: (1-255) 1
```

Next, give it the name of **group-1** with the *name* command:

```
>> Real server group 1# name
Current real server group name:
Enter new real server group name: group-1
```

Save and apply your changes.

VIPs

Alteon refers to VIPs as Virtual Servers. The nomenclature is different, but the concept is the same. This is where you will point all of the user traffic. The VIP menu is under */cfg/slb* as *virt*. As with the real servers and groups, there is a limited number available in Alteon's WebOS, which is 256 on the model used here:

```
>> Layer 4# virt 1
-------------------------------------------------------------
[Virtual Server 1 Menu]
      service - Virtual Service Menu
      vip      - Set IP addr of virtual server
      dname    - Set domain name of virtual server
      cont     - Set BW Contract
      layr3    - Enable/disable layer 3 only balancing
      ftpp     - Enable/disable FTP SLB parsing for virtual server
      ena      - Enable virtual server
      dis      - Disable virtual server
      del      - Delete virtual server
      cur      - Display current virtual configuration
```

```
>> Virtual Server 1#
```

To configure the IP address of the VIP, we'll use the *vip* command:

```
>> Virtual Server 1# vip
Current virtual server IP address: 0.0.0.0
Enter new virtual server IP address: 192.168.0.200
```

You also need to enable this virtual server:

```
>> Virtual Server 1# enable
Current status: disabled
New status:     enabled
```

```
>> Virtual Server 1#
```

With Alteon's WebOS, we need to enable one service at a time, based on the TCP/ UDP port required. There is a submenu called *service.* You will configure port 80 since we are setting this up for web service:

```
>> Virtual Server 1# service/
Enter virtual port: 80
-----------------------------------------------------------
[Virtual Server 1 http Service Menu]
       group   - Set real server group number
       rport   - Set real port
       hname   - Set hostname
       httpslb - Set HTTP SLB processing
       cont    - Set BW contract for this virtual service
       pbind   - Set persistent binding type
       udp     - Enable/disable UDP balancing
       frag    - Enable/disable remapping UDP server fragments
       nonat   - Enable/disable only substituting MAC addresses
       del     - Delete virtual service
       cur     - Display current virtual service configuration

>> Virtual Server 1 http Service#
```

You'll bind group 1, which contains real servers ws-1 through ws-4, to this service:

```
>> Virtual Server 1 http Service# group 1
Current real server group:
New pending real server group: 1

>> Virtual Server 1 http Service#
```

Check the status of the virtual server with the *cur* command:

```
>> Virtual Server 1# cur
Current virtual server 1:
   192.168.0.200, enabled, ftpp disabled
     virtual ports:
       http: rport http, group 1, frags
         real servers:
            1: 10.0.0.100,   weight 1,   enabled, backup none
            2: 10.0.0.101,   weight 1,   enabled, backup none
            3: 10.0.0.102,   weight 1,   enabled, backup none
            4: 10.0.0.103,   weight 1,   enabled, backup none
```

Apply and save the changes, and the VIP is configured. Point your browser to 192. 168.0.200 and you should get the load-balanced instance.

Redundancy

Configuring redundancy is essentially the same for both the flat-based and NAT-based network architectures. Alteon's WebOS employs VRRP to perform redundancy and does so on an IP-by-IP basis, instead of rendering the entire unit as active or standby. On both the active and the standby box, a Virtual Router (VR) is configured for every IP address that requires redundancy. A VR has an IP shared between two units, a Virtual Router ID (VRID), and a VRRP priority. The VRID identifies the virtual router to the other unit, and the VRRP priority determines which unit holds the VR on active or standby when both units are functioning. As with the VIPs and other configurations in WebOS, there is a finite number of VRs that can be used. The limit on the Alteon ACEDirector 184 used here is 255.

The configuration menu for VRRP is located at */cfg/vrrp*:

```
>> Main# /cfg/vrrp
-------------------------------------------------------------
[Virtual Router Redundancy Protocol Menu]
     vr       - VRRP Virtual Router Menu
     group    - VRRP Virtual Router Group Menu
     if       - VRRP Interface Menu
     track    - VRRP Priority Tracking Menu
     hotstan  - Enable/disable hot-standby processing
     on       - Globally turn VRRP ON
     off      - Globally turn VRRP OFF
     cur      - Display current VRRP configuration

>> Virtual Router Redundancy Protocol#
```

First, you must enable VRRP as a feature. To do this, just type:

```
>> Virtual Router Redundancy Protocol# on
Current status: OFF
New status:     ON

>> Virtual Router Redundancy Protocol#
```

Then set up a VRRP address of 192.168.0.10 to share between lb-1 and lb-2. This is critical for the flat-based architecture, since this is the default route for the servers. If this were NAT-based SLB, the IP would be 10.0.0.10 instead of 192.168.0.10. This is the default route for the servers, so no matter which unit is active, there will always be a default route ready. Select **vr** to configure the VR:

```
>> Virtual Router Redundancy Protocol# vr
Enter virtual router number: (1-256) 256
```

Assign it the number of 255, since this is going to be a default gateway. It doesn't matter what VR number we pick; you are just doing this for consistency. vip-1 will get VR number 1 to make things simpler:

```
-------------------------------------------------------------
[VRRP Virtual Router 256 Menu]
     track    - Priority Tracking Menu
     vrid     - Set virtual router ID
     addr     - Set IP address
     if       - Set interface number
     prio     - Set renter priority
     adver    - Set advertisement interval
     preem    - Enable/disable preemption
```

```
share   - Enable/disable sharing
ena     - Enable virtual router
dis     - Disable virtual router
del     - Delete virtual router
cur     - Display current VRRP virtual router configuration

>> VRRP Virtual Router 256#
```

First, assign a VRID number, again a number between 1 and 256. For consistency, give it 256, the same number as our VR number:

```
>> VRRP Virtual Router 256# vrid 256
Current virtual router ID:     1
New pending virtual router ID: 256

>> VRRP Virtual Router 256#
```

 Unless there is a specific reason to keep the numbers separate, keep the VR number and the VRID number the same, or else it can become very confusing.

Set the address as 192.168.0.10:

```
>> VRRP Virtual Router 256# addr 192.168.0.10
Current IP address:      0.0.0.0
New pending IP address: 192.168.0.10

>> VRRP Virtual Router 256#
```

Even though the interface defaults to 1, set it for 1 anyway, just to be sure:

```
>> VRRP Virtual Router 256# if 1
Current interface number:     1
New pending interface number: 1

>> VRRP Virtual Router 256#
```

If this is lb-1 (designated as the active box), assign it a VRRP priority of 200. If it is lb-2 (designated as standby), assign it a VRRP priority of 100. VRRP priority decides which box has the IP at any given moment. The active box with the highest number is the active box for that IP. The default is 100.

```
>> VRRP Virtual Router 256# prio 200
Current router priority:     100
New pending router priority: 200

>> VRRP Virtual Router 256#
```

The *preemptive* option decides whether the box will go to active status if faced with a partner that has a lower priority. For instance, if the primary box were to fail and then come up, *preemptive* would decide if the primary box would become active once it was functional again. If *preemptive* is disabled, the primary box remains as standby until the secondary unit fails:

```
>> VRRP Virtual Router 256# preem
Current preemption: enabled
Enter new preemption [d/e]: e

>> VRRP Virtual Router 256#
```

The *share* option decides whether box load balancers can share the same IP address. Since you are dealing strictly in an active-standby configuration, disable this feature (which is enabled by default):

```
>> VRRP Virtual Router 256# share
Current sharing: enabled
Enter new sharing [d/e]: d

>> VRRP Virtual Router 256#
```

Enable the VR, and you're finished:

```
>> VRRP Virtual Router 256# ena
Current status: disabled
New status:     enabled

>> VRRP Virtual Router 256#
```

Don't forget to apply and save the configuration for it to take effect.

Duplicate this process for the VIP, and if you are employing the NAT-based architecture, do so for the 10.0.0.1 shared IP address (the server's default gateway) as well. I recommend giving the VIP the VR number of 1 (and counting up from there) and the 10.0.0.1 IP address the VR number of 254 (counting down from 256). This just makes it easier to track.

Additional Features

This by no means covers all of the functions and capabilities of the Alteon series of load balancers. For additional configuration and features, refer to the Alteon documentation for your code.

9

Cisco's CSS
(Formerly ArrowPoint)
Configuration Guide

In June 2000, Cisco Systems, Inc. completed their acquisition of ArrowPoint Communications, Inc. They have since rolled the ArrowPoint switches into their product line as the CSS 11000 series of content switches.

Before the acquisition, ArrowPoint's line of products included the CS-50, CS-100 (old model), and the CS-150 in their pizza-box-style switches, as well as their CS-800 chassis-style switch. Now under the Cisco umbrella, they have been renamed the CSS series of switches with models including the CSS-11050, CSS-11150, and CSS-11800. The units are essentially the same hardware-wise and employ the same code. The changes, at least up to the publication time of this book, are largely cosmetic. Whether your switch says ArrowPoint or Cisco CSS, this chapter should apply to it.

When developing the configurations for this chapter, I used CSS-11150 (CS-150), running WebNS 4.0. Certain interfaces and commands may differ from the product you have because of differing code versions and hardware configurations. This product's specifications are:

> Vendor: Cisco Systems, Inc.
> Model: CSS-11150 (formerly the CS-150)
> Software Revision: WebNS 4.0.0
> Platform: Switch
> Ports: 8x, 10/100, Fast Ethernet, 2x Gigabit Ethernet

Cisco's CSS switches are somewhat of a melding of hardware-based switch SLB devices with some of the properties of the server-based units. Like their switch-based brothers, ArrowPoint switches are ASIC-based, relying on hardware to perform the load-balancing functions with all the speed advantages. They also employ a real-time OS, as with the other switches. One difference from the other switch-based devices, however, is that they contain hard drives. The hard drives contain the real-time OS, as well as the configuration files. This gives them added flexibility in storing many different software images, as well as different configuration files. In that respect, they are close to their server-based load-balancing cousins.

Introduction to the CLI

The Cisco CSS switches employ the Web Network Services (WebNS) real-time OS, as opposed to Cisco's IOS. WebNS is similar to the look and feel of IOS, but it is not the same. For instance, just as in IOS, the command *show run* will show the active configuration:

```
lb-1# show run
!Generated JUL 22 22:52:03
!Active version: ap0400000s

configure


!************************ INTERFACE ************************
interface ethernet-2
  bridge vlan 2

!************************* CIRCUIT *************************
circuit VLAN 1

  ip address 192.168.0.10 255.255.255.0

circuit VLAN 2

  ip address 10.0.0.1 255.255.255.0

lb-1#
```

Also, in Cisco's IOS, use the *config* command to initiate actual configuration changes:

```
lb-1# config
lb-1(config)#
```

This puts you into configuration mode the same as IOS, although with WebNS you don't need to specify t for terminal.

With WebNS, any change you make takes place immediately. The command *write mem* saves the current configuration in memory to the disk, so that the config at the next boot matches the current config:

```
lb-1# write mem
Working..(\) 100%
lb-1#
```

A better way to save the config, however, is with the command *save_config*. It not only saves the current configuration, but also archives the *startup-config* file in case something happens to the saved config:

```
lb-1# save_config
Working..(\) archive startup-config
lb-1#
```

Getting Started

One thing that may save you a lot of trouble in configuring a Cisco CSS switch is knowing that their serial ports employ a different pin-out configuration than standard serial connectors. They are even different than Cisco's standard rollover cable. You must use the RJ-45 adapters included with the switch, or adapters that are similarly wired. Cisco CSS switches usually come with one RJ-45 female to DB-9 female adapter and one RJ-45 to DB-25 female adapter. A null modem or Cisco rollover cable is not required. Use the following serial settings on your terminal program:

- 8 bits
- No parity
- 1 stop bit
- 9600 baud

Take the unit designated as the active unit (lb-1), plug into the serial console, and turn on the switch (lb-2, the redundant unit, will be configured afterwards). Log in with the NVRAM username and password (see the "Security" section for further explanation). If the unit is fresh from the factory, the default username is *admin*, and the password is *system*. If that account does not work, and you do not know the login and password, you can try the recover password procedure located in Appendix A.

If there is no previous configuration, you'll be prompted to run an initial startup script. Answer **n** to that question:

```
Username:admin
Password:******


##########################################################
##        Setup Script for the Content Smart Switch      ##
##########################################################


Checking for Existing Config...

No startup-config was found, continue with the setup script [y/n]? n
Exiting setup script.

CS150#
```

The first step is to set the environment of each of the load balancers so you know from the prompt into which you are logged:

```
CS150# prompt lb-1
lb-1#
```

This is only a user-based environment setting, not a global configuration, so this would need to be done for every user that logs in. To save this environment variable, use the *save_profile* command:

```
lb-1# save_profile
```

Use port 1 as the initial port—the port connected to the outside world. If you are using the NAT-based architecture, then also configure port 2. It is not important which ports are used, but for the purposes of this book, use ports 1 and 2.

To configure port 1's IP address, go into *conf* mode and choose circuit 1:

```
lb-1(config)# circuit VLAN 1
lb-1(config-circuit[VLAN 1])#
```

The prompt will reflect the change into circuit configuration. Circuits are Arrow-Point's term for Layer 3 interfaces, named by which VLAN they represent. Each VLAN can have only one circuit, so each circuit encompasses a VLAN. (It is possible, however, to have multiple subnets on a single VLAN/circuit.) Because of how the ArrowPoints handle redundancy, give the lead box an IP address of 192.168.0.10 instead of 192.168.0.11. In the "Redundancy" section, I will go into this further, but for now, give lb-1 an IP address of 192.168.0.10:

```
lb-1(config-circuit[VLAN 1])# ip address 192.168.0.10 255.255.255.0
lb-1(config-circuit-ip[VLAN 1-192.168.0.10])#
```

It's also a good idea to set a description of each VLAN. Since this is the outside network, designate this the "Outside network":

```
lb-1(config-circuit[VLAN 1])# description "Outside network"
```

As in IOS, the syntax is:

```
ip address [ IP address ] [ subnet mask ]
```

You can also append the IP address with a subnet prefix, such as:

```
lb-1(config-circuit[VLAN 1])# ip address 192.168.0.10/24
lb-1(config-circuit-ip[VLAN 1-192.168.0.10])#
```

Both methodologies end up with the same result.

Next, configure the default route to 192.168.0.1 using the *ip route* command:

```
lb-1(config)# ip route 0.0.0.0 0.0.0.0 192.168.0.1
```

The first two IP addresses are 0.0.0.0, the first representing the default route with a netmask of 0.0.0.0.

Now that basic networking is configured for the device, you should be able to log into it from the network. To complete the initial configuration, disable spanning-tree support, since you are using this switch only as a load balancer, not as a Layer 2 device:

```
lb-1(config)# bridge spanning-tree disabled
```

Duplicate that procedure on the second unit if you are using redundancy, and you are ready to proceed to either the flat-based or NAT-based architecture. Give lb-2 an IP address of 192.168.0.11, which will be changed to 192.168.0.10 later (again, this will be explained in the "Redundancy" section).

Security

Like IOS, WebNS has two different levels of access: read-only and superuser. Unlike IOS, WebNS allows you to create multiple accounts that are either superuser or read-only. In WebNS, you do not use the *enable* command. When you log in, you are already either a superuser or a read-only user. One and only one superuser account is stored in the switch's NVRAM, while other accounts are encrypted and stored in the configuration file.

To create a non-NVRAM superuser account, go into the *config* mode and use the command *username*. Remember not to use *username* in NVRAM.

```
lb-1(config)# username tony password test123
lb-1(config)#
```

This adds the user account **tony** with the password **test123**. If you want to give this account superuser privileges, then append that command with *superuser*:

```
lb-1(config)# username tony password test123 superuser
lb-1(config)#
```

Don't be concerned about storing the password as plain text in a configuration file. When you do a *show config*, you'll notice that the switch has automatically encrypted the password:

```
lb-1(config)# show run
!Generated JUL 22 23:45:48
!Active version: ap0400000s

configure


!*************************** GLOBAL ***************************
username tony des-password 5c6cecxydtgchbkg superuser
. . .
```

NVRAM Password

To change the NVRAM password, use the *username-offdm* command instead:

```
lb-1(config)# username-offdm admin password test123
```

When completed, the command will not show up in the configuration. The information is written only to the NVRAM.

> If you configure an account in the configuration file with the same username as that stored in NVRAM, the configuration file will override the NVRAM when you boot up the machine.

SSH

The Cisco CSS series supports the SSH protocol for command-line access. Connect using any standard SSH client. While Telnet is enabled by default, it's a good idea to use SSH exclusively. You can completely disable Telnet using the following command:

```
lb-1(config)# telnet access disabled
```

Starting with WebNS 4.0, a Cisco CSS switch requires a license to use SSH. Once entered, SSH will be configured and running. The default SSH configuration is sufficient security for just about all installations, so there isn't a need for adjustment. Version 3.x of WebNS, however, comes with SSH enabled and running by default.

> Because of older federal laws governing the export of encryption software, WebNS versions prior to 3.10 did not ship with support for the 3DES as an SSH encryption algorithm; only DES (often referred to as Single DES). Most Windows SSH clients support Single DES, but the popular SSH client for Unix does not have Single DES enabled by default. You can either use Telnet or recompile your SSH program to enable Single DES support. WebNS versions starting at 3.10 and later do not have this problem.

Flat-Based SLB

Following the blueprint from Chapter 6, you can now configure the Cisco CSS switch pair for a flat-based SLB implementation.

Thus far, lb-1 has been giving the IP address 192.168.0.10 and lb-2 the address 192.168.0.11. When redundancy is configured, the standby box's (lb-2) IP address is inactive and shares lb-1's IP of 192.168.0.10 (see Table 9-1). Do not configure the VIPs and real servers on both switches at this point, only on the active load balancer (lb-1). The configurations will be synced in the "Redundancy" section.

Table 9-1. lb-1 and lb-2 configuration; flat-based SLB

Unit	lb-1 (active)	lb-2 (standby)
IP address	192.168.0.10	192.168.0.11 (temp IP)
Subnet mask	255.255.255.0	255.255.255.0
Shared address	192.168.0.10	192.168.0.10
Default route	192.168.0.1	192.168.0.1

The subnet masks and default routes should have already been configured. Configure the web servers to their respective IP addresses as specified in the flat network architecture shown in Table 9-2.

Table 9-2. ws-1 through ws-4 IP configuration; flat-based SLB

Unit	ws-1	ws-2	ws-3	ws-4
IP address	192.168.0.100	192.168.0.101	192.168.0.102	192.168.0.103
Subnet mask	255.255.255.0	255.255.255.0	255.255.255.0	255.255.255.0
Default route	192.168.0.10	192.168.0.10	192.168.0.10	192.168.0.10
Service and port	HTTP:80	HTTP:80	HTTP:80	HTTP:80

Real Servers

The ArrowPoint term for real servers is "service." Creating one is very simple. Create the service with the *service* directive, give it an IP address, and make it active:

```
lb-1(config)# service ws-1
Create service <ws-1>, [y/n]:y
lb-1(config-service[ws-1])# ip address 192.168.0.100
lb-1(config-service[ws-1])# active
```

To see the status of the service, use the *show* command:

```
lb-1(config-service[ws-1])# show service ws-1

Name: ws-1              Index: 0
  Type: Local            State: Alive
  Rule ( 192.168.0.100  ANY  ANY )
  Redirect Domain:
  Keepalive: (ICMP  5   3   5 )
  Mtu:         1500      State Transitions:  0
  Connections:    0      Max Connections:    0
```

```
Total Connections: 0         Total Reused Conns: 0
Weight:            1         Load:                2

lb-1(config-service[ws-1])#
```

This display shows that the server is marked as **Alive**, which means it is answering to ICMP ping responses. In most cases, it is a good idea to see whether the web server is listening on port 80 and that it is actively responding to requests rather than just a ping check. To do this, add another directive:

```
lb-1(config-service[ws-1])# keepalive type http
```

When you run a *show service ws-1* again, you will see that the Cisco CSS is checking port 80 for a HTTP HEAD response. The HEAD request sends a "HEAD / HTTP/1.0" and looks for an OK response from the web server. If there is no OK response, the server is marked down. A server that is marked down will not receive live traffic.

```
lb-1(config-service[ws-1])# show service ws-1


Name: ws-1              Index: 0
 Type: Local            State: Alive
 Rule ( 192.168.0.100  ANY  ANY )
 Redirect Domain:
 Keepalive: (HTTP:HEAD:  5   3   5 )
 Mtu:            1500       State Transitions:  2
 Connections:       0       Max Connections:    0
 Total Connections: 0       Total Reused Conns: 0
 Weight:            1       Load:               2

lb-1(config-service[ws-1])#
```

If you do a *show config*, you will see the entire config for the new service:

```
. . .
!************************* SERVICE *************************
service ws-1
  ip address 192.168.0.100
  keepalive type http
  active
```

Repeat this process with the other web servers.

If at any point there is a need to take a server out of active rotation, you can do so with the *suspend* command. Go into the service's configuration (*service ws-1*, for instance) and simply type **suspend**:

```
lb-1(config)# service ws-1
lb-1(config-service[ws-1])# suspend
lb-1(config-service[ws-1])# show service ws-1


Name: ws-1              Index: 0
 Type: Local            State: Suspended
```

```
Rule ( 192.168.0.100  ANY  ANY )
Redirect Domain:
Keepalive: (HTTP:HEAD:    5   3   5 )
Mtu:                1500        State Transitions:  3
Connections:           0        Max Connections:    0
Total Connections: 0            Total Reused Conns: 0
Weight:                1        Load:               255

lb-1(config-service[ws-1])#
```

The configuration will look like this:

. . .

```
!*********************** SERVICE *************************
service ws-1
  ip address 192.168.0.100
  keepalive type http
  active

service ws-2
  ip address 192.168.0.101
  keepalive type http
  active
```
. . .

VIPs

WebNS has a slightly different concept of VIPs and groups. VIPs are organized under WebNS as "owners." Each owner can have its own VIP configured, which can come in handy when configuring many VIPs for different customers in a shared environment or other environments where it might be advantageous to group various VIPs. Each owner has individual instances known as "content rules," which is the ArrowPoint term for VIPs.

To create content rules (VIPs), there must be an owner. Create the owner "tony" using the *owner* command:

```
lb-1(config)# owner tony
Create owner <tony>, [y/n]:y
lb-1(config-owner[tony])
```

Once there is an owner, you can create the content rule named vip-1:

```
lb-1(config-owner[tony])# content vip-1
Create content <vip-1>, [y/n]:y
```

Set the VIP address to 192.168.0.200 with the *vip address* command:

```
lb-1(config-owner-content[tony-vip-1])# vip address 192.168.0.200
```

Add the real servers with the *add* command:

```
lb-1(config-owner-content[tony-vip-1])# add service ws-1
```

```
lb-1(config-owner-content[tony-vip-1])# add service ws-2
lb-1(config-owner-content[tony-vip-1])# add service ws-3
lb-1(config-owner-content[tony-vip-1])# add service ws-4
```

Only HTTP traffic should be load-balanced, so specify port 80 and the TCP protocol. This is crucial, otherwise all ports and protocols will be load-balanced, which is not usually a good idea as far as security is concerned.

```
lb-1(config-owner-content[tony-vip-1])# port 80
lb-1(config-owner-content[tony-vip-1])# protocol tcp
```

Now mark this content rule as active:

```
lb-1(config-owner-content[tony-vip-1])# active
```

Most changes to a content rule cannot be done while the rule is active, so if it's necessary to make a change to an active rule, you'll have to temporarily disable the service. This can be done with the *suspend* command:

```
lb-1(config-owner-content[tony-vip-1])# suspend
```

To show the VIP configurations, use the *show rule-summary* command:

```
lb-1# show rule-summary

VIP Address      Port  Prot Url                  CntRuleName     OwnerName  State
--------------   ----- ---- ------------------   --------------  ---------- ------
192.168.0.200    80    TCP                       vip-1           tony       Active

lb-1#
```

NAT-Based SLB

With the flat-based architecture, only port 1 of the Cisco switch is used. With the NAT-based architecture, port 2 is also used. Port 1 will be on VLAN 1, just as with the flat-based architecture and have the same 192.168.0.0/24 IP addresses. Port 2 will be located on VLAN 2 with the 10.0.0.0/24 IP addresses.

Thus far, lb-1 has been given the IP address 192.168.0.10 and lb-2 the address 192.168.0.11. When redundancy is configured, lb-2 will have the same IP address as lb-1, with the standby box's IP address inactive. This will also be true for VLAN 2. Configure lb-1 and lb-2 with separate IP addresses, which will be changed when redundancy is configured. With redundancy, lb-1 and lb-2 will have the IP address 10.0.0.1, with only one active at a given time.

To configure the additional VLAN and IP address, go into the interface configuration. In ArrowPoint, "interface" refers to switch ports. In this case, configure port 2, which the ArrowPoint refers to as interface Ethernet-2. Tag it as VLAN 2, which will create VLAN 2 on the switch. Note that VLAN is lowercase in this syntax:

```
lb-1(config)# interface ethernet-2
lb-1(config-if[ethernet-2])# bridge vlan 2
```

Now that VLAN 2 has been created, there is a circuit known as VLAN 2. You can configure this with an IP address as you did with circuit VLAN 1. Give it the name "Internal network":

```
lb-1(config)# circuit VLAN2
lb-1(config-circuit[VLAN2])# description "Internal network"
lb-1(config-circuit[VLAN2])# ip address 10.0.0.1 255.255.255.0
Create ip interface <10.0.0.1>, [y/n]:y
lb-1(config-circuit-ip[VLAN2-10.0.0.1])#
```

Note that in this particular syntax, VLAN2 is all one word. This is different than the syntax case in the *bridge* command, although they represent the same aspect of the configuration. This can become confusing if you are not careful.

Repeat this process on the lb-2, and you've completed preliminary configuration of the load balancers. Do not configure the VIPs and real servers on the standby unit (lb-2), because the configurations will be synced in the "Redundancy" section.

The configurations of VLAN 1 and VLAN 2 are shown in Tables 9-3 and 9-4.

Table 9-3. VLAN 1 configuration, NAT-based SLB

Unit	lb-1 (active)	lb-2 (standby)
IP address	192.168.0.10	192.168.0.11 (temp IP)
Subnet mask	255.255.255.0	255.255.255.0
Shared address	192.168.0.10	192.168.0.10
Default route	192.168.0.1	192.168.0.1

Table 9-4. VLAN 2 configuration, NAT-based SLB

Unit	lb-1 (active)	lb-2 (standby)
IP address	10.0.0.1	10.0.0.2 (temp IP)
Subnet mask	255.255.255.0	255.255.255.0
Shared address	10.0.0.1	10.0.0.1

The subnet masks and default routes should have already been configured. Configure the web servers to their respective IP addresses as specified in the NAT-network architecture as shown in Table 9-5.

Table 9-5. ws-1 through ws-4 IP configuration, NAT-based SLB

Unit	ws-1	ws-2	ws-3	ws-4
IP address	10.0.0.100	10.0.0.101	10.0.0.102	10.0.0.103
Subnet mask	255.255.255.0	255.255.255.0	255.255.255.0	255.255.255.0
Default route	10.0.0.1	10.0.0.1	10.0.0.1	10.0.0.1
Service and port	HTTP:80	HTTP:80	HTTP:80	HTTP:80

Real Servers

The ArrowPoint term for real servers is "service." Creating one is very simple. Create the service with the *service* directive, give the service an IP address, and make it active:

```
lb-1(config)# service ws-1
Create service <ws-1>, [y/n]:y
lb-1(config-service[ws-1])# ip address 10.0.0.100
lb-1(config-service[ws-1])# active
```

To see the status of the service, use the *show* command:

```
lb-1(config-service[ws-1])# show service ws-1


Name: ws-1                    Index: 0
  Type: Local                 State: Alive
  Rule ( 10.0.0.100  ANY  ANY )
  Redirect Domain:
  Keepalive: (ICMP   5   3   5 )
  Mtu:              1500      State Transitions:  0
  Connections:        0       Max Connections:    0
  Total Connections: 0        Total Reused Conns: 0
  Weight:            1        Load:               2


lb-1(config-service[ws-1])#
```

This display shows that the server is marked as **Alive**, which means it is answering to ICMP ping responses. In most cases, it is a good idea to see whether the web server is listening on port 80 and that it is responding to requests. To do this, add another directive:

```
lb-1(config-service[ws-1])# keepalive type http
```

When you do a *show service ws-1* again, you will see that the ArrowPoint is checking port 80 for a HTTP HEAD response. The HEAD request sends a "HEAD / HTTP/1.0" and looks for an OK response from the web server. If there is no OK response, the server is marked down. A down server does not receive traffic.

```
lb-1(config-service[ws-1])# show service ws-1


Name: ws-1                    Index: 0
  Type: Local                 State: Alive
  Rule ( 10.0.0.100  ANY  ANY )
  Redirect Domain:
  Keepalive: (HTTP:HEAD:   5   3   5 )
  Mtu:              1500      State Transitions:  2
  Connections:        0       Max Connections:    0
  Total Connections: 0        Total Reused Conns: 0
  Weight:            1        Load:               2

lb-1(config-service[ws-1])#
```

If you do a *show config*, you will see the entire config for the new service:

```
. . .
!*************************** SERVICE ***************************
service ws-1
  ip address 10.0.0.100
  keepalive type http
  active
```

If at any point there is a need to take a server out of active rotation, you can do so with the *suspend* command. Go into the service's configuration (*service ws-1*, for instance) and simply type **suspend**:

```
lb-1(config)# service ws-1
lb-1(config-service[ws-1])# suspend
```

You then see the service suspended with the *show* command:

```
lb-1(config-service[ws-1])# show service ws-1

  Name: ws-1                  Index: 0
    Type: Local               State: Suspended
    Rule ( 10.0.0.100  ANY  ANY )
    Redirect Domain:
    Keepalive: (HTTP:HEAD:   5   3   5 )
    Mtu:               1500      State Transitions:  3
    Connections:          0      Max Connections:    0
    Total Connections: 0         Total Reused Conns: 0
    Weight:               1      Load:               255

  lb-1(config-service[ws-1])#
```

Repeat this process with the other web servers, and you are ready to configure the VIPs.

VIPs

ArrowPoint's WebNS has a slightly different concept of VIPs and groups. VIPs are organized under what they call "owners." Each owner can have its own VIP configured, which can come in handy when configuring many VIPs for different customers in a shared environment or other environments where it might be advantageous to group various VIPs. Each owner has individual instances known has a "content rules," which is the ArrowPoint term for VIPs.

To create content rules (VIPs), there must be an owner. Create the owner "tony" using the *owner* command:

```
lb-1(config)# owner tony
Create owner <tony>, [y/n]:y
lb-1(config-owner[tony])
```

Once there is an owner, you can create the content rule named vip-1:

```
lb-1(config-owner[tony])# content vip-1
Create content <vip-1>, [y/n]:y
```

Set the VIP address to 192.168.0.200 with the *vip address* command:

```
lb-1(config-owner-content[tony-vip-1])# vip address 192.168.0.200
```

Add the real servers with the *add* command:

```
lb-1(config-owner-content[tony-vip-1])# add service ws-1
lb-1(config-owner-content[tony-vip-1])# add service ws-2
lb-1(config-owner-content[tony-vip-1])# add service ws-3
lb-1(config-owner-content[tony-vip-1])# add service ws-4
```

Only HTTP traffic should be load-balanced, so specify port 80 and the TCP protocol. This is crucial, otherwise all ports and protocols will be load-balanced, which is usually not a good idea as far as security is concerned.

```
lb-1(config-owner-content[tony-vip-1])# port 80
lb-1(config-owner-content[tony-vip-1])# protocol tcp
```

Now mark this content rule as active:

```
lb-1(config-owner-content[tony-vip-1])# active
```

The configuration will look like this:

```
. . .
!*************************** OWNER ***************************
owner tony

  content vip-1
    protocol tcp
    vip address 192.168.0.200
    add service ws-1
    add service ws-2
    add service ws-3
    add service ws-4
    port 80
```

Most changes to a content rule cannot be done while the rule is active, so to temporarily disable the rule, use the *suspend* command:

```
lb-1(config-owner-content[tony-vip-1])# suspend
```

To show the VIP configurations, use the *show rule-summary* command:

```
lb-1# show rule-summary

VIP Address      Port  Prot  Url                CntRuleName     OwnerName   State
---------------  ----- ----  ------------------ --------------  ----------  ------
192.168.0.200    80    TCP                      vip-1           tony        Active

lb-1#
```

The `Port` column is very important because it shows you what ports are answering.

> For security purposes, each VIP should have a port and protocol specified. You can check by using the *show rule-summary* command. If a VIP is listed as "Any" in the port column, then a port and protocol were not specified and any connection on any port will be load-balanced. This is a grave security risk in most situations. If you specify a port and protocol, only connections on the specified port and protocol will be forwarded; all other ports and protocols will be dropped.

Reverse NAT

In the previous configurations, connections from the Internet are allowed in, and the servers are permitted to respond. In certain cases, it may be necessary for individual web servers to be able to initiate outbound connections (this does not affect inbound connections). If the machines are on a public network, such as with flat-based SLB, this is no problem. But if the machines are sitting on RFC 1918 address space, they are incapable of initiating connections to the outside world. To fix this, you need to perform an outbound NAT, where the RFC addresses are NATed on the way out. Cisco calls this a "source group." To do this with the Cisco CSS switches, you'll need to specify a *group* directive. This WebNS concept of a group is different than the one explained in Chapter 2. The WebNS group concept pertains to outbound NAT. Create a vip-1 group to make sure the packets are translated on the way out:

```
lb-1(config)# group vip-1
Create group <vip-1>, [y/n]:y
lb-1(config-group[vip-1])# vip address 192.168.0.200
lb-1(config-group[vip-1])# add service ws-1
lb-1(config-group[vip-1])# add service ws-2
lb-1(config-group[vip-1])# add service ws-3
lb-1(config-group[vip-1])# add service ws-4
lb-1(config-group[vip-1])# active
```

With this configuration, if any of the individual web servers need to connect to the outside world, the outbound source address will be NATed to 192.168.0.200 and thus appear to come from that public IP address. The configuration will look like this:

```
. . .
!*************************** GROUP ***************************
group vip-1
  vip address 192.168.0.200
  add service ws-1
```

```
add service ws-2
add service ws-3
add service ws-4
active
```

If a group is not configured, then the real servers behind the load balancer will not be able to initiate connections to the Internet.

Redundancy

The Cisco CSS series of switches handles redundancy a bit differently from the other load balancers. With the Cisco CSS series, both units are configured almost identically, with one unit handling traffic while the other remains largely inactive. Because only one machine is active on the network, this presents a problem in how to administer the backup machine. I will go into detail with that problem later in this section. The Cisco CSS switches employ a modified VRRP protocol, running on a private interswitch link.

As of WebNS 4.0, the Cisco CSS series supports active-active configurations, but I will concentrate only on the active-standby configuration.

Thus far, both lb-1 and lb-2 have been given separate public IPs (192.168.0.0/24). If you are using the NAT-based SLB method, then you've configured them both for private IPs as well (10.0.0.0/24). The VIPs and real servers have not been configured on the standby (lb-2) unit. The next steps are to get the redundant protocol link running, and then sync up the two configurations.

Redundancy Protocol Link

To employ redundancy, you'll need to set up a private network between the two Cisco CSS switches. To do so, pick a port on each switch. For the purposes of this book, pick port 12. To prevent a potentially problematic bridging loop, set the ports and interfaces up first before you connect them with a crossover cable:

```
lb-1(config)# interface ethernet-12
lb-1(config-if[ethernet-12])# bridge vlan 3
lb-1(config-if[ethernet-12])#
```

Now configure the circuit with the newly created VLAN with an IP address and a description. Use the IP subnet of 172.16.0.0/24. It is an RFC 1918 address space and will have no access to the outside network. The switch lb-1 will be 172.16.0.1, and lb-2 will be 172.16.0.2. The only purpose of this network is to run a health-check protocol between the two switches:

```
lb-1(config-if[ethernet-12])# circuit VLAN 3
lb-1(config-circuit[VLAN 3])# description "Redundancy network"
lb-1(config-circuit[VLAN 3])# ip address 172.16.0.11/24
```

```
Create ip interface <172.16.0.11>, [y/n]:y
lb-1(config-circuit-ip[VLAN 3-172.16.0.11])#
```

Run a crossover cable between those two ports. A crossover cable is a Cat 5 cable with the TX and RX reversed, which enables a switch port to communicate with another switch port. When you connect the two, and they are powered up, you should see a link light if you have connected them correctly.

The following steps are for the active unit only (lb-1); the standby unit will be handled in a different manner.

To initiate redundancy, specify redundancy in the configuration. Since it's lb-1, also specify "master," because it will be the active box:

```
lb-1(config)# ip redundancy master
```

To sync the configurations between the two units, run a WebNS app session with the other unit. Now enable the app protocol:

```
lb-1(config)# app
```

Set the app peer as lb-2 (172.16.0.2):

```
lb-1(config)# app session 172.16.0.2
```

Now you are ready to set up the standby unit. Currently, it has the frontend IP of 192.168.0.11, but to become the standby unit, it must have the inactive IP of 192.168.0.10. There are three ways you can go about doing this:

1. Make the configuration changes via the serial console.

2. FTP the startup-config from lb-1 to a machine and edit the configuration. Upload it to the lb-2 and reboot.

3. Make the configuration changes via an additional administration interface that is not marked for redundancy. See the "Administration Network" section for more details.

If you are making the configuration changes via the serial console or an administrative interface, use the following instructions. If you are using FTP to upload a new config, follow the instructions in "Configuration file change."

Live machine redundancy setup

Set the units for app session peering, so the configurations sync. Enable app peering support:

```
lb-2(config)# app
```

Now set the app peer as lb-1 (172.16.0.1):

```
lb-2(config)# app session 172.16.0.1
```

Now set the standby unit for redundancy. Use the same *ip redundancy* command but without the *master* directive:

```
lb-2(config)# ip redundancy
```

Set up the redundancy protocol running between the two switches. This has already been set for the active switch:

```
lb-2(config)# circuit VLAN 3
lb-2(config-circuit[VLAN 3])# ip address 172.16.0.2/24
lb-2(config-circuit-ip[VLAN 3-172.16.0.2])# redundancy-protocol
lb-2(config-circuit-ip[VLAN 3-172.16.0.2])#
```

The next step is to configure the individual interfaces for redundancy. The only two interfaces that should be set for redundancy are VLAN 1 and, if you are using NAT-based SLB, VLAN 2:

```
lb-2(config)# circuit VLAN 1
lb-2(config-circuit[VLAN 1])# redundancy
```

With redundancy set, the IP addresses on the VLAN will become inactive since the unit is standby. You can now safely change the IP addresses to correspond with the IP address(es) on the active switch:

```
lb-2(config-circuit[VLAN 1])# no ip address 192.168.0.11
Delete ip interface <192.168.0.11>, [y/n]:y
lb-2(config-circuit[VLAN 1])# ip address 192.168.0.10/24
Create ip interface <192.168.0.10>, [y/n]:y
lb-2(config-circuit-ip[VLAN 1-192.168.0.10])#
```

 If you do not completely set redundany before this step, you will have two switches with the same active IP addresses, which will cause ARP problems on your network. You can use the *show redundancy* command to see if redundancy is indeed running before you proceed with re-IPing the interface.

To check the status of redundancy, use the command *show redundancy*:

```
lb-2(config)# show redundancy
Redundancy:              Enabled     Redundancy Protocol:       Running
Redundancy State:        Backup      MasterMode:                No
Number of times redundancy state changed to Master:            10
                                      to Backup:                11
Redundancy interface:    172.16.0.2
Current State Duration:  0 days 02:41:49
Last Fail Reason:        Other Switch Asserted Mastership
VRID:                    128         Priority:                  100
```

The first three fields are probably the most important. They show that redundancy is enabled, that the protocol is running, and the state is backup.

Syncing Configurations

Setting up initial redundancy may be fairly involved, but once it's taken care of, syncing the configuration from the active switch to the standby switch should be very simple. With the app sessions configured, most of the work is already done. Any changes made to the active switch should be pushed to the standby switch as soon as possible.

WebNS includes a script called *commit_redundancy* to automatically sync the switches. To run that script, use the following syntax:

```
lb-1# script play commit_redundancy "172.16.0.2 -a"
```

The script will produce the following output upon execution:

```
verifying app and redundancy configs ... \
Checking Backup app session up.... /
Checking redundancy state.... |
Working /
Commit successful!
lb-1#
```

If you encounter errors, make sure there is connectivity between the two switches on the redundancy link and ensure that the app session is configured correctly. A *–d* in the *commit_redundancy* command will set the script to debug mode, giving much more detailed output. Consult the documentation to find out more about this script.

Administration Network

Because of the way WebNS employs redundancy, it may be beneficial to have a separate network configured for administration purposes. The outside and internal networks are active only on the active switch. Because the network between the switches is used only for redundancy, there is no way to administer the standby switch. Configuring a separate interface and network for administration without redundancy configured will allow administration of both the active and standby devices.

For instance, configure VLAN 4 with an IP address of 172.16.1.1/24 for lb-1 and 172.16.1.2/24 for lb-2. If you put an administration machine on this network, you can log into both machines regardless of which is active. Port 11 is shown as an example here, but any available port will do. Be sure not to configure redundancy on this link.

```
lb-1(config)# interface ethernet-11
lb-1(config-if[ethernet-10])# bridge vlan 4
lb-1(config-if[ethernet-10])# circuit VLAN 4
lb-1(config-circuit[VLAN 4])# description "Administration network"
```

```
lb-1(config-circuit[VLAN 4])# ip address 172.16.1.1/24
Create ip interface <172.16.1.1>, [y/n]:y
lb-1(config-circuit-ip[VLAN 4-172.16.1.1])#
```

Additional Features

This by no means covers all of the functions and capabilities of the Cisco CSS series of load balancers. For additional configuration and features, refer to the ArrowPoint documentation for your version of code.

10

F5's BIG-IP

The F5 boxes are essentially modified Unix boxes, running a specialized version of BSDI Unix. Because of this, Unix command-line and account practices are in place. There is also a web-based interface, which, unlike the other products, is integral to how the device is configured. In this chapter I will make many references to the Web User Interface (WUI), whereas in other chapters the Command Line Interface (CLI) is the primary means of configuration.

There are two different types of accounts on the machine: the Unix user accounts and the WUI accounts. The only Unix user account configured by default is root, which has superuser status. Unix accounts only apply to the CLI. Multiple WUI accounts can be created with either read-only or superuser access. They apply only to the WUI.

Getting Started

Unlike the other products covered in this book, the F5 units require PC monitors for initial configuration. Although once initially configured they may be manipulated by command line and WUI, it's a good idea to keep a monitor or some sort of console access infrastructure handy in case of an emergency. Plug a monitor and keyboard into the unit (you will not need a mouse) and power one up. You will be asked a series of questions such as your time zone, the IP address you would like to give the F5 unit, etc. Once you input the answers, the box should boot up and leave you at a Unix login prompt.

When initially configuring the IP address of the device, use the guide shown in Table 10-1. If you are employing the flat-based architecture, use only the external interface (*exp0* for a Fast Ethernet port). If you are employing the NAT-based architecture, configure both the internal and external interfaces (*exp0* and *exp1* for Fast Ethernet).

Table 10-1. Flat-based SLB configuration

Unit	lb-1 (active)	lb-2 (standby)
IP address	192.168.0.11	192.168.0.12
Subnet mask	255.255.255.0	255.255.255.0
Shared address	192.168.0.10	192.168.0.10
Default route	192.168.0.1	192.168.0.1

Table 10-2 shows the configuration guidelines for NAT-based SLB.

Table 10-2. NAT-based SLB configuration

Unit	lb-1 (active)	lb-2 (standby)
IP address (VLAN 1)	192.168.0.11	192.168.0.12
Subnet mask	255.255.255.0	255.255.255.0
Shared address	192.168.0.10	192.168.0.10
Default route	192.168.0.1	192.168.0.1
IP address (VLAN 2)	10.0.0.2	10.0.0.3
Subnet mask	255.255.255.0	255.255.255.0
Shared address	10.0.0.1	10.0.0.1

If you are using redundant units, the initial configuration will ask you for the redundant units' IP addresses. You will also be asked for a root password (the password used for CLI access) and for a username and password for administration purposes, which will be the WUI account.

WUI Administration

When you've completed the initial configuration on both machines, you can log in via SSH or the WUI. For configuration purposes, the WUI is best. To access the WUI, you'll need a browser with SSL support. SSL is a secure version of the HTTP protocol. Like SSH, it involves encryption for command-line access. Nothing goes over the network as plain text, and everything is encrypted, so it is safe for administrative use. Type the IP address (or domain name if you have DNS configured) into the browser, and be sure to use the *https://* prefix, which denotes a secure HTTP SSL connection. For example, the URL for lb-1 would be *https://192.168.0.11.*

When you first log in, you'll most likely receive a dialog box from your browser asking you to verify connections to this site. The reason is that the F5 box employs the SSL protocol. The SSL protocol typically relies on an SSL certificate generated by a certificate authority such as Verisign. The certificate usually costs money, around $400 (U.S.), depending on the circumstances. This step ensures the reliability and safety of a secure site, such as with a web store. For the purposes of configuring your BIG-IP boxes, however, a certificate is unnecessary. Therefore, you'll just use an unsigned certificate authority, that being the BIG-IP box. This will generate warnings with your browser. However, you can ignore them and move on.

Here is what the browser says about the unsigned certificate used for the SSL interface:

```
This Certificate belongs to:
  lb-1.labs.vegan.net
  Support
  Vegan
  New York, New York, USA


                      This Certificate was issued by:
                        lb-1.labs.vegan.net.back
                        Support
                        Vegan
                        New York, New York, USA


  Serial Number: 00
  This Certificate is valid from Wed Sep 06, 2000 to Fri Aug 28, 2037
  Certificate Fingerprint:
    B5:8F:F2:A1:94:99:6B:49:BA:77:5D:AA:9B:48:FC:49
```

All this information corresponds to the questions that you answered during the initial configuration.

The first time you log into the SSL interface, you'll have to go through a few windows on your browser to accept the new certificate. After that, each time you quit your browser, restart it, and log back in, you'll be asked to accept the certificate. This is normal and not indicative of any security problems.

When the SSL certificate is accepted, the initial screen will look like Figure 10-1.

To configure the device, click on the link labeled "Configure your BIP/ip Controller." This will bring you to the menu shown in Figure 10-2.

This is the main menu for configuration. If you are logged in as a superuser, you'll see the Apply and Reset buttons at the bottom. If you are a read-only user, then you will not see the buttons and, of course, will have no ability to change the configuration.

From this window, you can learn a lot about the status of the SLB device. This screen shows you the name of the unit, the version of BIG-IP software employed, the load-balancing method, whether the unit is active or standby, and much more.

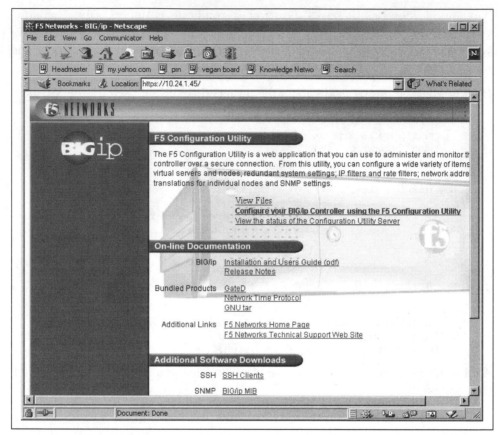

Figure 10-1. F5's BIG-IP

On the left of the screen, you'll see a menu of configurable options. These menus
are:

Virtual Servers

This is the VIP configuration menu.

Nodes

This is the real server configuration menu.

NATs

This menu allows direct NAT setup from one network to another, which is
very useful in a NAT-based networking setup.

Secure NATs

This menu allows the configuration of one or many NATs. This is where one
public IP address is used as the source address for multiple private machines.
Again, this is very useful for the NAT-based network architecture.

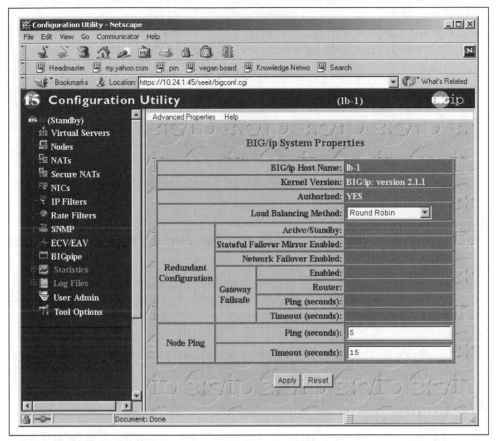

Figure 10-2. Configuration utility menu

NICs

> This is the Network Interface Card (NIC) configuration menu. This is where you may modify primary IP addresses (not VIPs) on the various interfaces.

IP Filters

> This is the IP filter configuration menu. It allows you to generate IP filters (or ACLs) to protect your real servers. These may be useful in specific networking situations.

Rate Filters

> This allows you to limit the amount of bandwidth going to different VIPs or real servers.

SNMP

> This is the SNMP configuration menu.

ECV/EAV

Extended Content Verification (ECV) and Extended Application Verification (EAV) are the methods by which you can ensure that your web servers are responding correctly.

BIGpipe

BIGpipe is a CLI command used for various configuration and statistics-gathering tasks. There is a web interface for this command in this menu, which allows you to access the command from the browser.

Statistics

These are basic statistics that the BIG-IP generates, such as memory, system, and VIP.

Log Files

This provides a look into some of the Unix-based log files, such as */var/log/ messages*.

User Admin

This allows you to manage the WUI accounts on your system. You can add, delete, and modify user access privileges.

Tool Options

This allows you to change how items are displayed. There are various changeable options in the WUI interface.

CLI Administration

The CLI interface is still very useful on the BIG-IP for certain quick tasks and some of the more down-and-dirty activities. The SSH server was configured upon initial setup, so all you need to do is log in as the user root:

```
[~] root@zorak(pts/0)
[5:49pm]# ssh root@192.168.0.11
root@192.168.0.11's password:
Last login: Wed Sep  6 10:25:24 2000 from 192.168.0.250

Copyright 1996, 1997, 1998, 1999 F5 Networks, Inc. , Seattle, Washington,
U.S.A. All rights reserved.

F5 Networks, Inc. is a registered trademark, and BIG/ip is a trademark of F5
Networks, Inc. Other product and company names are registered trademarks or
trademarks of their respective holders.

BY USING THIS SOFTWARE YOU AGREE THAT YOU HAVE READ THIS LICENSE AND ANY
OTHER RELEVANT LICENSE(S), THAT YOU ARE BOUND BY ALL TERMS AND THAT IT IS
THE ONLY AGREEMENT BETWEEN US, SUBJECT TO AMENDMENTS, REGARDING THE
SOFTWARE AND DOCUMENTATION. PLEASE NOTE THAT YOU MAY NOT USE, COPY, MODIFY
OR TRANSFER THE PROGRAM OR DOCUMENTATION OR ANY COPY, EXCEPT AS EXPRESSLY
PROVIDED BY AGREEMENT.
```

```
For technical support contact:

     e-mail:          support@f5.com
     toll-free:       1 (888) 88-BIGIP
     voice:           (206)  505-0800
     fax:             (206)  505-0801
```

```
lb-1:~#
```

This is a standard Unix bash shell with all the functionality you would expect. If you are familiar with the Unix environment, then your favorite commands such as *ps*, *top*, and *ls*, are at your disposal. There is also an SSH client, allowing you to SSH into the partner unit or another pair altogether. (I wouldn't go SSHing around to any system from the BIG-IPs, nor would I use the account as an all-purpose Unix shell; there isn't any immediate security problem with doing that, but it's still not a good idea.)

Two of the most important BIG-IP implemented commands are: *bigtop* and *bigpipe*. *bigtop* is a statistics-reporting tool, similar to Unix's *top*. *bigpipe* is a general command that controls various aspects of the SLB functionality. *bigtop* is a great way to check out the statistics of a given VIP or real server (node).

Flat-Based SLB

With the initial configuration, the external network interface has already been set up. You have two load balancers, lb-1 and lb-2, each with a primary IP and both sharing a single IP as shown in Table 10-3.

Table 10-3. Flat-based configuration

Unit	lb-1 (active)	lb-2 (standby)
IP address	192.168.0.11	192.168.0.12
Subnet mask	255.255.255.0	255.255.255.0
Shared address	192.168.0.10	192.168.0.10
Default route	192.168.0.1	192.168.0.1

You are now ready to configure the SLB services. With the BIG-IPs, a VIP must exist before a real server can be configured, so add the VIPs first. Click on Virtual Servers and you should get a menu such as the one shown in Figure 10-3.

All you need to input is the address and port; the asterisks indicate that you can leave those fields blank. Click on Add to make the addition. To add the real servers, click on the Nodes menu. From there, you can click on the Add Node button at the top to add the remainder of the nodes. You should then be all set for the flat-style load-balancing method.

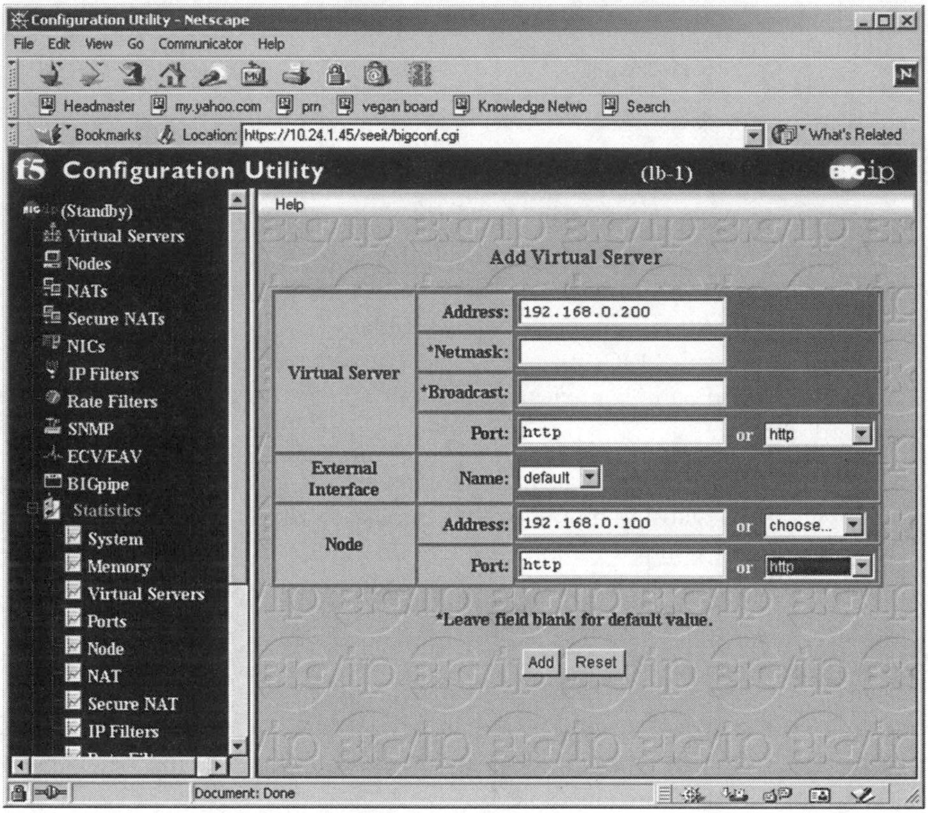

Figure 10-3. Virtual Servers menu

NAT-Based SLB

To configure the NAT-based SLB implementation, both the external and internal interfaces must be configured for IP addresses. For our example, they are configured as shown in Table 10-4.

Table 10-4. NAT-based configuration

Unit	lb-1 (active)	lb-2 (standby)
IP address (VLAN 1)	192.168.0.11	192.168.0.12
Subnet mask	255.255.255.0	255.255.255.0
Shared address	192.168.0.10	192.168.0.10
Default route	192.168.0.1	192.168.0.1
IP address (VLAN 2)	10.0.0.2	10.0.0.3
Subnet mask	255.255.255.0	255.255.255.0
Shared address	10.0.0.1	10.0.0.1

With the BIG-IPs, a VIP must exist before a real server can be configured, so click on the Virtual Servers menu and add the VIPs first. All you need to input is the address and port. Click on Add to make the addition. To add the rest of the real servers, click on the Nodes menu. From there, you can click on the Add Node button at the top to add the remainder of the nodes. You should then be all set for the NAT-style load-balancing method.

Redundancy

Redundancy between the two units is handled one of two ways: through the network or through a serial fail-over cable. The BIG-IPs can detect if the other unit has failed, or even if there isn't any network traffic on the active unit. There are several options for failure detection and fail-over between the boxes; check the documentation for details.

The configuration files are synced through SSH. SSH allows you to set what is known as a "host key" for the other unit. This allows you to log into the partner unit without a password over SSH. The SSH server checks the key sent by the client, and if they match, the connection is established without a password. This is how you check to see if sync is configured correctly—by logging into the partner unit via SSH without a password:

```
lb-1:/usr/sbin# ssh lb-2
Last login: Fri Sep  8 22:17:29 2000 from 10.24.1.62

Copyright 1996-2000 F5 Networks, Inc. , Seattle, Washington, U.S.A.
All rights reserved.

F5 Networks, Inc. and BIG/ip are registered trademarks of F5 Networks,
Inc. Other product and company names are registered trademarks or
trademarks of their respective holders.

BY USING THIS SOFTWARE YOU AGREE THAT YOU HAVE READ THE LICENSE AND ANY
OTHER RELEVANT LICENSE(S), THAT YOU ARE BOUND BY ALL TERMS AND THAT IT IS
THE ONLY AGREEMENT BETWEEN US, SUBJECT TO AMENDMENTS, REGARDING THE
SOFTWARE AND DOCUMENTATION. PLEASE NOTE THAT YOU MAY NOT USE, COPY, MODIFY
OR TRANSFER THE PROGRAM OR  DOCUMENTATION OR ANY COPY, EXCEPT AS EXPRESSLY
PROVIDED BY AGREEMENT.

        For technical support contact:

                e-mail:        support@f5.com
                toll-free:     1 (888) 88-BIGIP
                voice:         (206)   505-0800
                fax:           (206)   505-0801

No mail.
Terminal type? [vt100]
Terminal type is vt100.
lb-2:~#
```

To fail-over from one unit to the other, you can either use the WUI or the CLI. With the WUI, the command is on the main page of the active unit. You can only fail the active unit to the standby and not send the command to the standby unit to become active. On the CLI, the command is *bigpipe fo slave* on the active unit. For example:

```
lb-1:/usr/sbin# bigpipe fo slave
```

 Do not use the command *bigpipe fo master* on the slave unit. This will cause serious ARP problems and will likely cause a network interruption on your VIPs. Only issue the *bigpipe fo* command on the active unit.

To sync the configurations between two boxes, use the command on the main page of the WUI. It will take only a few seconds to complete.

Stateful Fail-Over

The BIG-IP unit allows you to perform what is called "stateful fail-over." Stateful fail-over is when the active unit shares TCP session and persistence table information with the standby unit. Under circumstances in which the pair does not share information, persistence information is lost, and all of the TCP sessions will be reset, which is a problem if the traffic is HTTP downloads or FTP-related. With stateful fail-over enabled, all that information is shared. Even if the active box dies, the TCP sessions will remain active and persistence will be preserved. This feature can be enabled as a radio button on the main page of the WUI.

11

Foundry ServerIron Series

The Foundry Networks, Inc. ServerIron series of load balancers falls into the switch family of products. They have (at the time of publication) the ServerIron series of stackable switches and their BigServerIron chassis series of switch/router/load balancers. Foundry ServerIrons are capable of being the Layer 2 switches that interconnect the servers. However, in this chapter they operate only as load balancers attached to a Layer 2 infrastructure. I used model ServerIronXL, code revision IronWare 07.0.07T12.

Foundry switches are incorporated into a network a little differently than the other load balancers we've discussed. In a flat-based network, they operate in a bridge-path, two-armed configuration rather than in a route-path, one-armed configuration. For NAT-based networks, they operate in a one-armed configuration. This setup may change in later versions of the code, but as of 7.0.0, this is the scenario.

Foundry ServerIrons are completely solid state, with no moving parts. As a result, they take only a few seconds to boot or reboot. Their configurations and software images are stored in a flash RAM, again with no moving parts. You can store two software images, as well as two configuration images. To see what is in your flash RAM, use the command *show flash*:

```
SSH@foundry1#show flash
Code Flash Type: AMD 29F016, Size: 32 * 65536 = 2097152, Unit: 2
Boot Flash Type: ATMEL 29C010A, Size: 1024 * 128 = 131072
Compressed Primary Code size = 1301986, Version 07.0.01T12
Compressed Secondary Code size = 1301986, Version 07.0.01T12
Boot Image Version 06.00.00
SSH@foundry1#
```

Command Line Interface (CLI)

The CLI for the Foundry series of load balancers is very similar to Cisco's IOS. When you first log into a ServerIron, you are in a read-only environment. Just like IOS, you need to enable the account to become a superuser in order to make changes to the system and configurations. Any configuration change you make takes effect immediately. If the current configuration is to remain in effect when the unit is power cycled, a *write mem* command must be issued.

There are three basic modes of user administration with ServerIron's IronWare: the read-only mode, the enable mode, and the config mode. When you initially log in, you'll get the read-only mode. The *enable* command will get you into superuser mode, and to make configuration changes, *conf term* will get you into config mode. To start off with configuration, you'll need a female DB9 straight-through cable connection to your serial device. Set your terminal emulation program for the following settings:

    8 bits
    No parity
    1 stop bit
    9600 baud

Connect and hit Enter a few times, and you should get this prompt:

```
ServerIron>
```

As with Cisco's IOS, the default login (denoted by the > at the end of the prompt) is not an account that can make changes. You need to enable in order to make configuration changes:

```
ServerIron>enable
No password has been assigned yet...
ServerIron#
```

You'll get a prompt that ends in #, which denotes that you are in *superuser* mode.

Hostname

It's always a good idea to give any network device a hostname, if for no other reason than to know into which machine you are logged. The Foundry OS Iron-Ware puts the hostname in the prompt, making it easier. To give the device a hostname, go into *conf term* mode and use the *hostname* command:

```
ServerIron#conf t
ServerIron(config)#hostname lb-1
lb-1(config)#
```

Don't forget to do a *write mem* to save the configuration changes.

Password

You should definitely configure a password at this point, to keep things secure. It should be configured through the console connection, rather than Telnet. Unless you are using SSH or are positive about the network environment from which you telnet, you should only change passwords via the console connection.

The following command will make your superuser password *admin* (you should really pick something else for your password, of course):

```
lb-1(config)#enable superuser-password admin
```

You'll also want to set the Telnet password and authentication for when network connectivity is configured. The following command will set the Telnet password to *admin* (which again, you should change to something other than your enable password):

```
lb-1(config)#enable telnet password admin
```

To enable Telnet password authentication, use the following command:

```
lb-1(config)#enable telnet authentication
```

 Enabling Telnet authentication is important; otherwise, anyone telneting to the ServerIron will automatically be dropped into a non-privileged shell without being asked for a password. Anyone with access to your IP can get information on your configuration, or if they have the enable password, change into superuser mode.

Network Configuration

The next step is to get the device up on the network. With either the flat-based or NAT-based network architecture, the initial network configuration will apply for both. Assume that you are using port 1 of the switch. You are going to configure the device with the IP information shown in Table 11-1.

Table 11-1. ServerIron IP configuration

Unit	lb-1 (active)	lb-2 (standby)
IP address	192.168.0.10	192.168.0.11
Subnet mask	255.255.255.0	255.255.255.0
Default route	192.168.0.1	192.168.0.1

The IP configuration for the ServerIron is very easy. Make sure that you are in *conf term* mode and the following commands will take care of all the IP information:

```
lb-1(config)#ip address 192.168.0.10 255.255.255.0
lb-1(config)#ip default-gateway 192.168.0.1
```

To add DNS servers, use the *ip dns* command. For example, lets take the DNS server addresses of 208.185.43.205 and 208.185.43.206:

```
ip dns server-address 208.185.43.205 208.185.43.206
```

The *ip dns server-address* command allows you to specify more than one DNS address.

If all is configured correctly, you should now be able to telnet into the switch. However, see the section "SSH Configuration" if you have an SSH client. This is a much more secure way of accessing a ServerIron because the passwords and commands are encrypted.

SSH Configuration

The Foundry ServerIron series, as of the 7.0 releases, supports SSH access for command-line administration. This should be used whenever possible. Remember to use the console port to configure SSH unless you are 100% sure of your network surroundings and that no one is snooping during your Telnet session to get passwords. To configure SSH, go into the *enable* and *conf term* modes. To enable the RSA key, you'll need to give the machine a domain:

```
ip dns domain-name vegan.net
```

Of course, substitute for **vegan.net** whatever your domain name is. If you don't have a domain, make something up, since this is a requirement for SSH (it needs a domain name for the SSH public key). It is usually not critical what you put in for the domain name, although you should use the same name that your other equipment uses, just to keep things tidy.

Now you can generate the RSA key needed for SSH encryption. Just to be safe, let's erase any existing RSA key and do a *write mem*:

```
lb-1(config)#crypto key zeroize rsa
lb-1(config)#write mem
```

Now lets generate the key:

```
lb-1(config)#crypto key generate rsa
```

The process will take about a minute.

```
Generating rsa key pair............................................................
...................................................................................
..........................done!
```

```
rsa public_key "1024 37
16497602174403911166153355737403434785228304834580534978998637925677399511194412239
580361864968528683258995869053052354425464551516081013231328282382286208474108794
63674923734368989568049501474927647434121777264295209540717336445236133646981082106
22032318998918857576903449891522965999309640222221113350677717 lb-1@vegan.net"

rsa private_key "*************************"
telnet@lb-1(config)#
```

Don't forget to do a *write mem*:

```
lb-1(config)#write mem
```

SSH is now enabled on your system. Before you can log in, however, you'll need to create accounts that allow access, since SSH requires a username to log in. To do this, use the *username* command:

```
lb-1(config)#username admin privilege 0 password admin
```

The syntax to the username command is: **username**, **privilege** (0 stands for read-write or superuser; 4 stands for port config; 5 stands for read-only), **password**. The account created with the previous command made a username of *admin*, with a password of *admin*. That account is capable of making any change on the system.

To enable this type of local authentication, the command is:

```
aaa authentication login default local
```

SSH will now work. If you are using a Unix client to log in, the process looks like this:

```
[~] tony@zorak(pts/1)
[5:09pm]# ssh admin@192.168.0.11
Host key not found from the list of known hosts.
Are you sure you want to continue connecting (yes/no)? yes
Host '192.168.0.11' added to the list of known hosts.
admin@192.168.0.11's password:
SSH@lb-1>
```

When you are logged in via SSH, you are not automatically enabled as superuser. You must *enable* to become superuser and make any changes:

```
SSH@lb-1>enable
Password:
SSH@lb-1#
```

Flat-Based SLB

Most of the network configuration has already been presented in the "Getting Started" section, so there isn't much more prep work needed. For flat-based SLB to work on a Foundry ServerIron, you must have the ServerIron in the Layer 2 path of traffic. This is a flat-based, bridge-path, two-armed connection. With these steps complete, you are now ready to configure the VIPs and real servers.

Real Servers

Configuring the real servers is very simple. First, definer a real server with a name and IP address:

```
SSH@lb-1(config)#server real ws-1 192.168.0.100
```

This will bring your prompt to a hierarchical system under which configuration changes for this real server can be made. The prompt will reflect what server configuration you are in:

```
SSH@lb-1(config-rs-ws-1)#
```

You must define what port or ports this real server will use. Since you are dealing with web servers, port 80, or port http, will accomplish the same thing:

```
SSH@lb-1(config-rs-ws-1)#port http
```

And now you are done with the configuration for ws-1. Repeat these steps for ws-2 through ws-4.

VIPs

To configure a VIP, first define it with a name and IP address. You can pick any name you wish, such as vip-1, or even a domain name such as *www.vegan.net.* Go with vip-1, since that is the configuration method being used:

```
server virtual vip-1 192.168.0.200
```

This will bring you into the same type of hierarchical menu as with real servers:

```
SSH@lb-1(config-vs-vip-1)#
```

Define which ports are associated with this VIP. Again, since you are dealing with web servers, use port http:

```
SSH@lb-1(config-vs-vip-1)#port http
```

You need to bind the real servers to the VIP. You can bind them one at a time or all at once. The syntax for the *bind* command is somewhat complicated; you specify a port on the virtual server, then a real server, then a port on that real server:

```
SSH@lb-1(config-vs-vip-1)#bind http ws-1 http
```

This binds the HTTP port of ws-1 to the HTTP port of the virtual server. Repeat this step with ws-2 through ws-3, and the configuration is complete. Point your browser to the VIP's IP address and you should get the web pages.

NAT-Based SLB

The NAT-based network architecture is a bit more complicated than the flat-based architecture and is slightly different than other load balancers. With a ServerIron, use a route-path, one-armed network. Both the private and public networks are on the same LAN, so there is no need to set up VLAN on the switch.

Private network default route

Configure the 10.0.0.0/24 network to act as the default route for the servers. You need to set the NAT source address so servers in the internal network have a default route:

```
SSH@lb-1(config)#server source-ip 10.0.0.1 255.255.255.0 192.168.0.1
```

This will route all traffic through the load balancer on the way out. Everything is complete on the network site, and you are ready to configure your real servers and VIPs.

Real Servers

Configuring the real servers is very simple. First, define a real server with a name and IP address:

```
SSH@lb-1(config)#server real ws-1 10.0.0.100
```

This will bring your prompt to a hierarchical system under which configuration changes for this real server can be made. The prompt will reflect what server configuration you are in:

```
SSH@lb-1(config-rs-ws-1)#
```

You must define what port or ports this real server will use. Since you are dealing with web servers, port 80, or port http, will accomplish the same thing:

```
SSH@lb-1(config-rs-ws-1)#port http
```

You are finished with the configuration for ws-1. Repeat these steps for ws-2 through ws-4.

VIPs

VIP configuration is also very simple. To configure a VIP, first define it with a name and IP address. You can pick any name you wish, such as vip-1, or even a domain name such as *www.vegan.net*. Here we'll use vip-1, in accordance with the configuration method:

```
server virtual vip-1 192.168.0.200
```

This will bring you into the same type of hierarchical menu as with real servers:

```
SSH@lb-1(config-vs-vip-1)#
```

You must define what ports are associated with this VIP. Again, since you are dealing with web servers, use port http:

```
SSH@lb-1(config-vs-vip-1)#port http
```

Bind the real servers to the VIP. You can bind them one at a time or all at once. The syntax for the *bind* command is somewhat complicated; you specify a port on the virtual server, then a real server, then a port on that real server:

```
SSH@lb-1(config-vs-vip-1)#bind http ws-1 http
```

This binds the HTTP port of ws-1 to the HTTP port of the virtual server. Repeat this step with ws-2 through ws-3, and the configuration is complete. Point your browser to the VIP's IP address and you should get the web pages.

Redundancy

Foundry ServerIrons employ their proprietary protocol known as Hot Standby Redundancy. To implement this, configure lb-1 as you did earlier. The unit lb-2 will be configured later. First, select a switch port to act as a private link between the two devices. This is what the protocol will run over. Let's select port 3, since you've used port 1, and if you are using NAT-based architecture, then you'll have used port 2 as well. You'll need to get the MAC address of the default route port of the web servers. If you are using the flat-based architecture, it is port 1; if you are using NAT-based architecture, then it is port 2. You can get the command by running *show interface*:

```
SSH@lb-1(config)#show interface e 1
FastEthernet1 is up
  Hardware is FastEthernet, address is 00e0.5205.8016 (bia 00e0.5205.8016)
  Configured speed auto, actual 100Mbit, configured duplex fdx, actual fdx
  Member of L2 VLAN ID 1, port is untagged, port state is FORWARDING
  STP configured to ON, priority is high, flow control enabled
  mirror disabled, monitor disabled
  Not member of any active trunks
  Not member of any configured trunks
  No port name
  5 minute input rate: 1264 bits/sec, 2 packets/sec, 0.00% utilization
  5 minute output rate: 29856 bits/sec, 5 packets/sec, 0.02% utilization
  4522245 packets input, 555055486 bytes, 0 no buffer
  Received 411078 broadcasts, 0 runts, 5 giants
  5 input errors, 0 CRC, 0 frame, 0 ignored
  749024 multicast
  7758222 packets output, 3940407493 bytes, 0 underruns
  0 output errors, 0 collisions
SSH@lb-1(config)#
```

Use the flat-based architecture for now and get the MAC address of 00e0.5205.8016 for this particular switch port.

To mark this port as redundant and to set up the protocol, use the following command:

```
SSH@lb-1(config)#server backup ethernet 1 00e0.5205.8016
```

With this configuration, one switch will be active while the other switch will be inactive, not forwarding IP or Layer 2 traffic.

To get lb-2 configured, copy the config from lb-1 to lb-2, changing only the 192. 168.0.11 address to 192.168.0.12. Do a *write mem*, and then reload the switch. Assuming it is the secondary unit, the switch will boot up and see that it is indeed the secondary unit.

To show redundancy status, use the command *show server backup*:

```
SSH@lb-1(config)#show server backup
```

IV

Appendixes

A

Quick Command Guide

This appendix provides a quick reference to commonly performed administration tasks involving the load balancers featured in this book. It is designed to save time and help in a crisis situation, when reading through a chapter would take too long. The quick command guide assumes you have set up the SLB units in a manner consistent with the examples and network architectures detailed in this book; however, these commands should work in most other circumstances as well. The syntax and information are based on the software and hardware versions of the products at the time of writing and may vary depending on your version.

Alteon (WebOS)

These commands are based on WebOS Version 8.0.x, but most will apply to newer versions and the earlier 6.0.x releases. Unless specified, all changes need to have an *apply* done to make them effective. Shortcuts can be used where needed. For example, */info/vrrp* can be shortened to */i/vrrp*.

Reboot switch   `/boot/reset`

Fail-over status   `/info/vrrp`

Default to original factory config

Enter:

    `/boot/conf factory`

Then reset the switch.

Take a real server out of production temporarily

Use */oper/slb/dis [server number]*, such as */oper/slb/dis 4*, to disable real server 4 temporarily.

Put a suspended real server back in production

Use */oper/slb/ena [*`server number`*]* such as */oper/slb/ena 4*, to enable real server 4.

Fail-over to standby unit

There is no easy way to fail-over units with Alteons unless the VRRP priorities on both boxes are the same (which is a bad idea). There are two choices. First, you can change the VRRP priorities on the standby unit to a higher value than the active unit. This can be quite tedious, especially if you have many VRRP entries configured.

```
/cfg/vrrp/vr 1/prio 50
/cfg/vrrp/vr 2/prio 50
/cfg/vrrp/vr 3/prio 50
```

Alternatively, you can unplug all network connections to the active Alteon unit. The backup unit will then take over.

Change admin password

The default admin account password is *admin*. To change it, use the command:

```
/cfg/sys/user/admpw
```

Show status of real servers

To show which real servers are up or down, use the following command:

```
/info/slb/dump
```

This will dump all of the real, group, and virtual server stats. The first entries will be the stats for the real server:

```
Real server state:
  1: ws-1, 00:d0:b7:66:9a:10, vlan 1, port 1, health 4, up
  2: ws-2, 00:d0:b7:66:9a:6f, vlan 1, port 1, health 4, up
  3: ws-3, 00:d0:b7:66:9a:77, vlan 1, port 1, health 4, up
  4: ws-4, 00:d0:b7:66:9a:5a, vlan 1, port 1, health 4, up
```

Show software version

The command */info/sys* will give you the version of code that is currently running:

```
>> Main# /info/sys
System Information at  0:17:09 Sun Sep 10, 2000

ACEswitch 184
sysName:
sysLocation:
Last boot: 14:12:49 Tue Aug 29, 2000 (reset from Telnet)

MAC address: 00:60:cf:45:9d:60    IP (If 1) address: 0.0.0.0
Hardware Revision: B
Hardware Part No: C05_5A-D_6A-D
Software Version 8.0.39 (FLASH image2), active configuration.


>> Information#
```

Foundry ServerIron Series (IronWare)

These configurations apply to IronWare Version 7.0 and, most likely, later versions as well. All changes take effect immediately, but a *write mem* is needed to save them to flash so they are active upon the next boot.

Reboot switch   `reload`

Fail-over status   `SSH@lb-1(config)# show server backup`

Default to original factory config

To go back to the original factory config, use the command *erase startup-config* and reload the switch. It will come back up with a blank configuration and no password:

```
ServerIron# erase startup-config
```

Take a real server out of production

To take a real server out of production, first go into the virtual server in which the real server is enabled, and then issue the *no* command to take the real server (ws-1 in this case) out of rotation:

```
SSH@lb-1(config)# server virtual vip-1
SSH@lb-1(config-rs-vip-1)# no bind http ws-1 http
```

If you'd prefer to make that real server unavailable for all VIPs, simply unconfigure the real server outright:

```
SSH@lb-1(config)# no server real ws-1
```

Put a suspended real server back in production

To add an already configured real server (back) into production, go into the virtual server menu and add the server:

```
SSH@lb-1(config)# server virtual vip-1
SSH@lb-1(config-vs-vip-1)# bind http ws-1 http
```

And the real server is back in production.

Fail-over to standby unit

The best way to fail-over to a standby is to reboot (or power-cycle) the active unit. The standby unit will become active and won't become standby again unless the now-active unit fails.

Change admin password

The default password for the login and superuser accounts is null, so it should be set as soon as possible:

```
lb-1(config)# enable superuser-password admin
```

Recovery of a lost password

If you've lost the superuser password for a ServerIron and have console access to the device, you can recover the password. Plug a serial connection into the switch and hit Enter a few times to make sure you've got an active connection. Then power-cycle the switch:

```
Enter 'b' to go to boot monitor ...
BOOT MONITOR>
```

Then type "no password" and hit Enter:

```
BOOT MONITOR> no password
OK! Skip password check when the system is up.
```

Then give the command *boot system flash primary* and hit Enter. This will boot the unit.

```
BOOT MONITOR> boot system flash primary
BOOT INFO: load from primary copy
BOOT INFO: code decompression completed
BOOT INFO: branch to 04001500
...
```

The system will boot up and you will get a read-only prompt. Type **enable** and you'll be in the privileged-enable mode, where you can reset the superuser password:

```
ServerIron>enable
No password has been assigned yet...
ServerIron#
```

Show status of real servers

To show the status of a given real server, use the command *show server real* followed by the name of the real server (or leave this blank for info on all of the real servers):

```
SSH@lb-1# show server real ws-1
Real Servers Info

Name : ws-1                                    Mac-addr: 0800.20c0.7bb0
IP:192.168.0.100       Range:1    State:Active       Wt:1    Max-conn:1000000
Src-nat (cfg:op):(off:off)    Dest-nat (cfg:op):(off:off)
Remote server   : No          Dynamic : No       Server-resets:0
Mem:server: 02009eae Mem:mac: 0458ef00
```

Port	State	Ms	CurConn	TotConn	Rx-pkts	Tx-pkts	Rx-octet	Tx-octet	Reas
http	active	0	0	0	0	0	0	0	0
default	unbnd	0	0	0	0	0	0	0	0
Server	Total		0	0	0	0	0	0	0

Show status of VIPs

To show the status of a given VIP, use the command *show server virtual* followed by the name of the virtual server (or leave this blank for info on all of the virtual servers):

```
SSH@lb-1# show server virtual vip-1
Virtual Servers Info
```

```
Server Name: vip-1          IP : 192.168.0.200      :   1
Status: enabled  Predictor: least-conn  TotConn: 0
Dynamic: No      HTTP redirect: disabled
                 Intercept: No
ACL: id =   0
Sym: group =  1 state =  5 priority =   0 keep =   0
 Activates =    1, Inactive= 0
Port     State      Sticky  Concur  Proxy      CurConn   TotConn   PeakConn

http     enabled    NO      NO      NO            0         0         0
default  enabled    NO      NO      NO            0         0         0
```

Show software version

To show the version of the software you are running, use the command *show version*:

```
SSH@lb-1#show version
  SW: Version 07.0.07T12 Copyright (c) 1996-1999 Foundry Networks, Inc.
     Compiled on Jul 28 2000 at 11:35:12 labeled as SLB07007
  HW: ServerIron Switch, serial number 058016
  400 MHz Power PC processor 740 (revision 8) with 32756K bytes of DRAM
   24 100BaseT interfaces with Level 1 Transceiver LXT975
    2 GIGA Fiber uplink interfaces, SX
  256 KB PRAM and 8*2048 CAM entries for DMA 0, version 0807
  256 KB PRAM and 8*2048 CAM entries for DMA 1, version 0807
  256 KB PRAM and 8*2048 CAM entries for DMA 2, version 0807
  256 KB PRAM and 1*2048 CAM entries for DMA 4, version 0104, SEEQ GIGA MAC 8100
  256 KB PRAM and 1*2048 CAM entries for DMA 5, version 0104, SEEQ GIGA MAC 8100
  128 KB boot flash memory
 4096 KB code flash memory
 2048 KB BRAM, BM version 10
  128 KB QRAM
  512 KB SRAM
Octal System, Maximum Code Image Size Supported: 1965568 (0x001dfe00)
The system uptime is 17 days 21 hours 26 minutes 51 seconds

SSH@lb-1#
```

Cisco's WebNS (ArrowPoint)

The following commands are for Version 4.0 and later, but most will work with earlier versions. All changes take effect immediately but must be saved to take effect upon rebooting.

Reboot switch   reboot

Fail-over status   show redundancy

Default to original factory config

To restore to the *no config*, you must clear out the *running-config* (the configuration in memory) as well as the *startup-config* (the configuration on the disk):

```
lb-1# clear running-config
running-config will be permanently lost.  Continue, [y/n]:y
```

```
Clearing(\) 100%
lb-1# clear startup-config
startup-config will be permanently lost.  Continue, [y/n]:y
lb-1#
```

If you have used the *save_config* command, you must also execute the *clear archive startup-config* command:

```
lb-1# clear archive startup-config
```

Then reboot the machine. When it comes back up, it will have no configuration and will prompt you to use the startup configuration script. Log in with the username and password configured in the NVRAM.

Take a real server out of production temporarily

To take a real server out of service, go into *conf* mode and the real server's configured service. Then give the *suspend* command:

```
lb-1(config)# service ws-1
lb-1(config-service[ws-1])# suspend
lb-1(config-service[ws-1])# show service ws-1
```

With a *show service ws-1*, we see that the state is now suspended:

```
Name: ws-1                Index: 1
  Type: Local             State: Suspended
  Rule ( 192.168.0.100  ANY  ANY )
  Redirect Domain:
  Keepalive: (ICMP   5   3   5 )
  Mtu:            1500        State Transitions:  1
  Connections:       0        Max Connections:    0
  Total Connections: 1        Total Reused Conns: 0
  Weight:            1        Load:               255

  lb-1(config-service[ws-1])#
```

Put a suspended real server back in production

To add a real server back into production, go into *conf* mode and the real server's configured service. Simply give the *active* command, and the real server is restored into load-balancing rotation:

```
lb-1(config)# service ws-1
lb-1(config-service[ws-1])# active
lb-1(config-service[ws-1])#
```

Fail-over to standby unit

On the standby unit, issue the command *redundancy force-master*. This will make the standby unit temporarily active. To switch back, use the same command on the old active unit (now standby), or the command *ip redundancy master*.

Change admin password

There is no single administrator superuser account; any account can have superuser access. There are two places where ArrowPoint keeps username and password information: in the NVRAM and in the configuration file (encrypted).

In the NVRAM, only one account is stored, and it is always superuser. It will not show up in the configuration file. If an account of the same username is added in the configuration file, it will supercede the password in the NVRAM. To change or add a non-NVRAM account, go into *config* mode and use the *username* command:

```
lb-1(config)# username tony password test123
```

If you want the account to have superuser access, append the command with *superuser*. Even if you are just changing an existing user's password, you still need to specify *superuser*, or else the account will become a nonsuperuser account:

```
lb-1(config)# username tony password test123 superuser
```

To change the NVRAM password, use the *username-offdm* command:

```
lb-1(config)# username-offdm admin password test123
```

The command does not appear in the configuration. The information is written only to the NVRM.

Recovery of a lost password

The NVRAM account is the only account that you can change when you can't log in as an administrative user. To do this, boot the machine up with a serial cable attached. You'll be given the chance during the boot-up process to exit into the Offline Diagnostic Monitor menu by hitting any key:

```
BootRom...


Fast Boot - Skipping DIAGS - BOOTING

Reading configuration records...OK
Checking previous shutdown..OK
Initializing the disk...OK

Press any key to access the Offline Diagnostic Monitor menu...
```

Doing so will bring you to this menu:

```
Transferring to menu...



        CS-150 Offline Diagnostic Monitor menu, Version: 4.00 Build 3

        M A I N   M E N U

        Enter the number of a menu selection:

        1*      Set Boot Configuration
        2.      Show Boot Configuration
        3*      Advanced Options
        4.      Reboot System

   >
```

Select option 3, which will bring you to this menu:

```
Enter the number of a menu selection:

1.       Delete a Software Version
2*       Security Options
3*       Disk Options
r.       Return to previous menu


>
```

Select option 2:

```
CS-150 Offline Diagnostic Monitor menu, Version: 4.00 Build 3

S E C U R I T Y   O P T I O N S

Enter the number of a menu selection:

1.       Set Password Protection for Offline Diagnostic Monitor
2.       Set Administrative Username and Password
r.       Return to previous menu


>
```

Option 2 of this menu will prompt you to change the administrator username and password:

```
Enter <administrator> username (Minimum 4 characters): tony
Enter <administrator> password:
Confirm <administrator> password:
```

The active configuration file will supercede any existing account, so be sure to create or change the password of an account that does not exist in the configuration file. When the unit boots up again, you will be able to log in as an administrator.

Show status of real servers

Use the command *show service* on a given real server or the command by itself to list the status of all real servers:

```
lb-1# show service ws-1

Name: ws-1              Index: 1
 Type: Local            State: Alive
 Rule ( 192.168.0.100  ANY  ANY )
 Redirect Domain:
 Keepalive: (ICMP   5   3   5 )
 Mtu:             1500     State Transitions:  0
 Connections:     0        Max Connections:    0
 Total Connections: 0      Total Reused Conns: 0
 Weight:          1        Load:               2

lb-1#
```

Show status of VIPs

To show the status of a VIP, use the *show rule-summary* command:

```
lb-1# show rule-summary

VIP Address      Port  Prot Url                  CntRuleName     OwnerName  State
---------------  ----- ---- ------------------   --------------  ---------- ------
192.168.0.100    80    TCP                       ws-1            tony       Active

lb-1#
```

The command doesn't allow you to specify any particular VIP; it gives info on all configured VIPs.

F5's BIG-IP

The following configurations apply to F5's BIG-IP.

Reboot switch   `reboot`

Fail-over status

The fail-over status can be found on either the main page of the WUI or with the command *bigpipe fo*:

```
lb-1:~# bigpipe fo
BIG/ip is in STANDBY failover state
```

Default to original factory config

Log in via SSH and delete */etc/hosts*:

```
lb-1:~# rm /etc/hosts
```

Then reboot the box and the unit will come up the same as when it came from the factory, awaiting a fresh config.

Take a real server out of production temporarily

From the main menu on the left, select Node and then the node of the real server you want to disable. There is an Enable checkbox; simply uncheck the box and click Apply.

Put a suspended real server back in production

From the main menu on the left, select Node and then the node of the real server you want to reenable. Check the Enable checkbox and click Apply.

Fail-over to standby unit

This can be done through either the WUI or the CLI. On the WUI of the active unit (not possible on the standby unit), click on the Make Standby button on the main page. With the CLI, use the following command on the active unit:

```
lb-1:~# bigpipe fo slave
```

Do not issue the command *bigpipe fo master* on the standby unit or issue a WUI command to the slave to become master. This will most likely cause serious ARP problems with the VIPs, resulting in a VIP outage. If the master machine is still active, it should be told to become slave, rather than the slave told to become master.

Change admin password

There are two types of accounts on the BIG-IP: the WUI and the CLI. In the WUI, use the User Admin menu to change passwords and administer accounts. For the CLI, use the Unix command *passwd*:

```
lb-1:~# passwd
Changing local password for root.
New password (128 significant characters):
Retype new password:
passwd: updating passwd database
passwd: done

lb-1:~#
```

B

Direct Server Return Configuration

The purpose of this appendix is to provide configuration examples for the setup of Direct Server Return (DSR) on various operating systems. As stated earlier, DSR is a way for outbound traffic to bypass the load balancer, sending traffic directly to the default router of that subnet. This can represent significant time savings. Not all SLB devices support DSR, and some have limitations on the types of features that are compatible with DSR, so check your vendor's documentation. This appendix is meant to serve as a general guide; different vendors may implement slightly different variations of DSR. Many vendors also have different names for DSR, such as nPath™ with F5's BIG-IP and SwitchBack™ with Foundry's Server-Iron, so keep that in mind.

DSR uses the loopback interface on a machine to spoof the address of the VIP on the load balancer when sending traffic out, making it look as if the load balancer sent the packet instead of the server, thus eliminating the need for the load balancer to process that traffic. The loopback interface is a special kind of network interface inside the machine. Usually, it is used only by the operating system for internal network communications, but it can be used for other purposes, such as DSR.

Generally, there are four necessary steps for the configuration of DSR:

1. Configure the IP alias on the server's loopback interface with the IP address of the VIP on the load balancer.

2. Configure the server to bind to both the real IP address (may be necessary so the load balancer can still perform health checks) and the new loopback IP address.

3. Point the default route directly towards the router (rather than through the load balancer).

4. Configure the load balancer to enable DSR.

IP Loopback Configuration

The first step is OS-specific. We've included the necessary steps to configure the loopback interface for Linux (tested with the 2.2 kernel, which should work with other versions), Solaris (tested with Solaris 7, which should also work with other versions), and Windows 2000. If you are using another operating system, check your documentation if you are unsure of how to configure the loopback address. We'll use the IP address of 192.168.0.200 to represent the VIP address and 192.168.0.100 to represent the real IP of the server.

Solaris Loopback Configuration

On a Solaris machine, if you run an *ifconfig –a* command (the Unix command to show information on all network interfaces), you'll get something similar to the following output:

```
[tony@vegan]# ifconfig -a
lo0: flags=1000849<UP,LOOPBACK,RUNNING,MULTICAST,IPv4> mtu 8232 index 1
        inet 127.0.0.1 netmask ff000000
hme0: flags=1000843<UP,BROADCAST,RUNNING,MULTICAST,IPv4> mtu 1500 index 2
        inet 192.168.0.100 netmask ffffff00 broadcast 192.168.0.255
        ether 8:0:20:c0:7b:b0
[tony@vegan]#
```

You need to create an additional `lo0` interface. To do this, plumb it first with the Unix *ifconfig* command. In Solaris, IP aliases for an interface are appended with a ":x", where x is the number of the IP alias. Since this is the first IP alias we are adding to the loopback interface, we'll give it the name `lo0:1`:

```
[tony@vegan]# ifconfig lo0:1 plumb
```

Now when you run *ifconfig –a*, it will show the lo0:1 interface:

```
lo0:1: flags=1000848<LOOPBACK,RUNNING,MULTICAST,IPv4> mtu 8232 index 1
        inet 0.0.0.0 netmask 0
```

Give the newly created interface the IP address of the VIP configured on the load balancer, 192.168.0.200. Don't forget to include the appropriate netmask information.

```
[tony@vegan]# ifconfig lo0:1 192.168.0.200 netmask 255.255.255.0 up
```

Now the *ifconfig –a* command will show the configured interface:

```
lo0:1: flags=1000849<UP,LOOPBACK,RUNNING,MULTICAST,IPv4> mtu 8232 index 1
        inet 192.168.0.200 netmask ffffff00
```

The loopback interface is now configured for DSR. If you have more than one VIP serviced by this server, you can add as many extra loopback interfaces as you require.

Linux Loopback Configuration

On a Linux machine, the *ifconfig –a* command will show something similar to this:

```
[tony@vegan]# ifconfig -a
eth0      Link encap:Ethernet  HWaddr 00:D0:B7:66:99:4A
          inet addr:192.168.0.100  Bcast:192.168.0.255  Mask:255.255.255.0
          UP BROADCAST RUNNING MULTICAST  MTU:1500  Metric:1
          RX packets:6079071 errors:0 dropped:0 overruns:0 frame:0
          TX packets:1177762 errors:0 dropped:0 overruns:12 carrier:0
          collisions:0 txqueuelen:100
          Interrupt:9 Base address:0xde80

lo        Link encap:Local Loopback
          inet addr:127.0.0.1  Mask:255.0.0.0
          UP LOOPBACK RUNNING  MTU:3924  Metric:1
          RX packets:40794 errors:0 dropped:0 overruns:0 frame:0
          TX packets:40794 errors:0 dropped:0 overruns:0 carrier:0
          collisions:0 txqueuelen:0

[tony@vegan]#
```

The interface `eth0` is the Ethernet interface, while `lo` is the loopback interface. To create an additional `lo` interface (an IP alias), we'll use the *ifconfig* command. Like Solaris, additional IP addresses on a physical interface are appended with an ":x", where x is the number of the additional interface. For the first alias, we'll use `lo:1`:

```
[tony@vegan]# ifconfig lo:1 192.168.0.200 netmask 255.255.252.0
```

Make sure you have the IP aliases compiled as options in the kernel. If you don't, you'll get an error when attempting to bring one up.

This is all that is required to add an IP alias to a Linux loopback interface. An *ifconfig –a* command shows the new loopback interface:

```
lo:1      Link encap:Local Loopback
          inet addr:192.168.0.200 Mask:255.255.255.0
          UP LOOPBACK RUNNING  MTU:3924  Metric:1
```

The loopback interface is now configured for DSR. If you have more than one VIP serviced by this server, you can add as many extra loopback interfaces as you require.

Windows 2000

Setting up a loopback interface is much more complicated with Windows 2000 than with Linux or Solaris. By default, Windows 2000 does not typically come installed with a loopback interface, so you must add one. Here are the steps necessary:

1. Go into the Control Panel and select Add/Remove Hardware.

2. Click on Add/Troubleshoot a device, then select Next.

3. Windows will probably try to find some new hardware. Just wait until you get to the next menu, which will be a list of hardware Windows has detected.

4. Click on Add a new device and then select Next.

5. You'll get a prompt asking to have Windows search for new hardware. You'll want to select the No, I want to select... option.

6. There will be a list of hardware types; select Network adapters.

7. There will be a list of manufacturers; select Microsoft. The only adapter available will be the Microsoft Loopback Adapter. Select that and then Next, and Next again to install the adapter.

8. When it is complete, click on Finish.

9. Go into the Control Panel window and select Network and Dialup Connections. Windows has probably named the new loopback adapter something like "Local Area Connection 2." It's a good idea to rename it something more appropriate, like "Loopback Interface."

10. Click on Properties for the Loopback Interface, then on TCP/IP Properties, which will bring up the screen shown in Figure B-1. Give it the IP address of 192.168.0.200 (the IP address of the VIP).

The loopback interface is now ready for DSR. If you have more than one VIP serviced by this machine, you can click on Advanced in the TCP/IP properties of the Loopback Interface and add additional IPs.

Web Server Configuration

Once the loopback interface on a server has been configured, the web server (or other type of server) must be set to listen to that loopback interface. As an example, let's take Apache, the popular open source web server. This would be part of an Apache configuration for a non-DSR-configured web server:

```
<VirtualHost 198.168.0.100>
    ServerAdmin tony@vegan.net
    DocumentRoot /www/docs/
    ServerName www1.vegan.net
    ErrorLog logs/error_log
    CustomLog logs/access_log common
</VirtualHost>
```

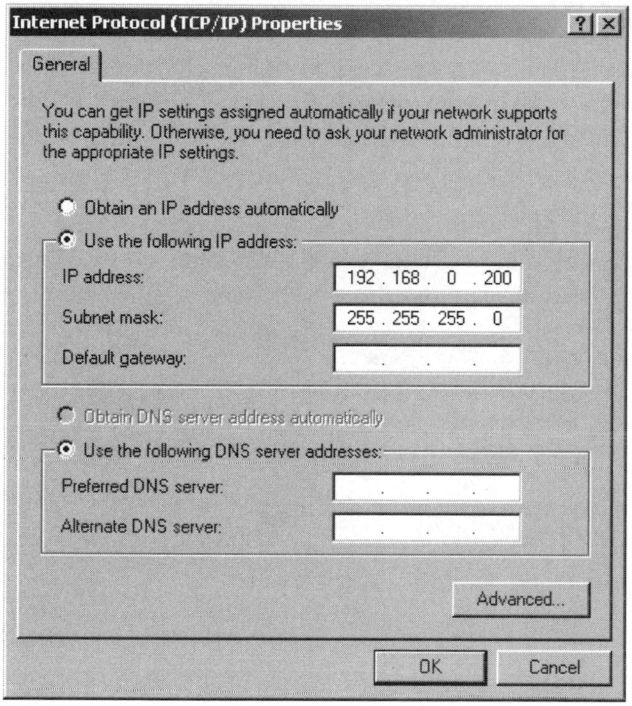

Figure B-1. TCP/IP properties in Windows 2000

With DSR enabled, we would also add the following configuration to listen to the loopback interface:

```
<VirtualHost 198.168.0.200>
    ServerAdmin tony@vegan.net
    DocumentRoot /www/docs/
    ServerName www1.vegan.net
    ErrorLog /www/logs/error_log
    CustomLog /www/logs/access_log common
</VirtualHost>
```

It is a good idea to configure both 192.168.0.200 and 192.168.0.100, even though they are essentially duplicates. This is so the load balancer can perform health checking on the 192.168.0.100 interface, and so you can browse the server individually without going through the load balancer, while the 192.168.0.200 instance provides DSR functionality.

This is just an example. Your web or other server configuration may vary depending on software and version.

Layer 3 Path

To ensure that the traffic isn't unnecessarily hitting the load balancer on the way out, make sure the default route path doesn't pass through the load balancers. To do this, just change the default route of the servers to point to the router on the subnet, rather than to the load balancer.

DSR does not generally work with bridge-path, because there can be only one path for Layer 2 traffic in and out, which is through the load balancer. Enabling DSR does not bypass the load balancer with bridge-path. Doing so would defeat the purpose.

C

Sample Configurations

The purpose of this appendix is to provide a quick reference guide to the multitude of possible load-balancing configurations and implementations available. All diagrams are vendor-neutral, and a specific product may require slight changes. Not all vendors will support all configurations, so be sure to check the manual or the vendor if you are not sure.

Virtually all load balancing can be classified by using this simple matrix in Figure C-1:

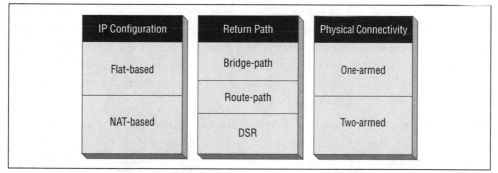

Figure C-1. An SLB implementation matrix

Each configuration falls under one of each of the three columns. Not all combinations work, but this matrix should greatly simplify how load-balancing implementations are classified and represented no matter what product is used.

All of the figures presented here involve redundancy so that any unit in the configuration could fail without an interruption of service. Redundancy in a given scenario can often depend on the other equipment in a configuration, so keep in mind that these figures do not represent the only way to achieve full redundancy.

Flat-Based Topologies

Flat-based scenarios involve IPs of the VIPs and real servers on the same subnet. They are so named because of the flat-type subnet topology they use. Figure C-2 shows the possible scenarios available with the flat-based topology in white, with variations that don't work in gray.

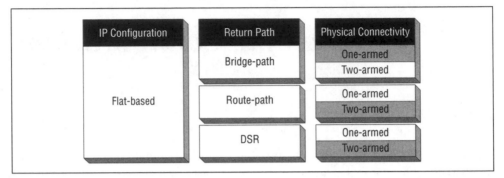

Figure C-2. A flat-based matrix

There are two primary methods for implementing flat-based SLB: bridge-path and route-path.

Flat-Based, Bridge-Path, Two-Armed

The configuration shown in Figure C-3 is common with the switch-based load balancers. It involves the load balancer in the Layer 2 path of the return traffic. This type of configuration utilizes flat-based SLB exclusively, not allowing for any type of NAT-based configuration. Redundancy is an issue because there cannot be more than one Layer 2 path in the configuration. One load balancer must be inactive and must not forward Layer 2 traffic.

The default route for the servers is the IP address on the router, where access is provided to the Internet, so there is no need for a floating IP between the load balancers other than VIP addresses. This type of configuration is not compatible with Direct Server Return (DSR). The load balancers act as a Layer 2 bridge between two separate LANs, while both LANs occupy the same IP address space.

Flat-Based, Route-Path, One-Armed

The type of configuration shown in Figure C-4 is similar to the previous setup because both utilize flat-based SLB and sit on just one subnet. In this case, however, the load balancer uses the route-path method because it is in the Layer 3 return for the traffic as the server's default route. The load balancer's default route

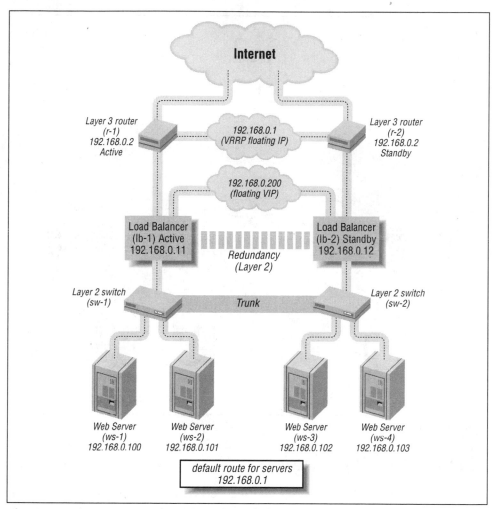

Figure C-3. A flat-based, bridge-path, two-armed SLB implementation

is the router sitting on the subnet, which provides connectivity to the Internet. The load balancer connects to the Layer 2 infrastructure with only one connection.

Flat-Based DSR, One-Armed

The scenario in Figure C-5 is exactly like the flat-based, route-path, one-armed SLB implementation except that outbound server traffic does not pass through the load balancer, only inbound. This setup is not compatible with most cookie-based persistent configurations nor with any Layer 5–7 URL hashing/rewriting configurations. The servers have the VIP address of the load balancer configured on their loopback interfaces, and their default route is the router sitting on the subnet. This bypasses the load balancer for outbound traffic.

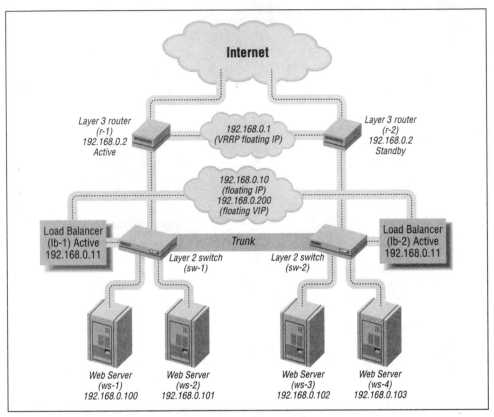

Figure C-4. A flat-based, route-path, one-armed SLB implementation

NAT-Based Topologies

On NAT-based SLB, IPs of the VIPs and real servers are on separate subnets with the load balancer performing NAT. It is so named because of the NAT from one subnet to another. Figure C-6 shows the possible combinations available in a NAT-based SLB configuration in white, with those that are not possible in gray.

NAT-based SLB does not work with bridge-path because it requires Layer 3 functionality to perform the NAT.

NAT-Based, Route-Path, Two-Armed

The NAT-based configuration shown in Figure C-7 involves the load balancer performing NAT between two subnets, usually a publicly routable subnet and a private nonrouted (RFC 1918) subnet. The load balancer sits on two VLANs, with one connection into each. The default route for the servers is the shared IP address on the active load balancer on the private network (VLAN 2).

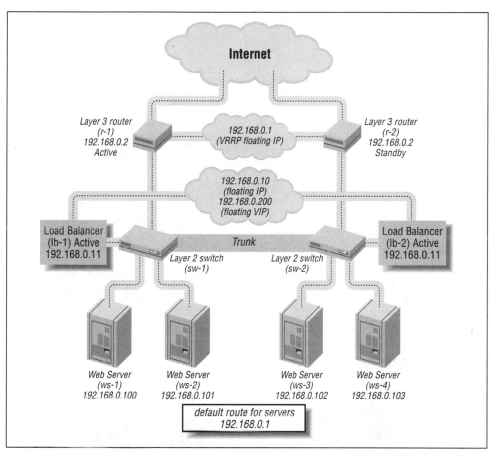

Figure C-5. A flat-based, one-armed DSR implementation

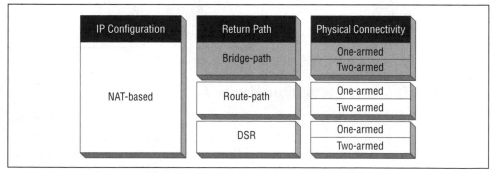

Figure C-6. A NAT-based matrix

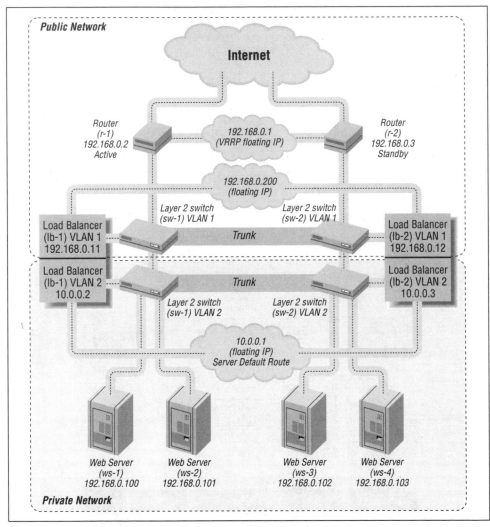

Figure C-7. A NAT-based, route-path, two-armed SLB implementation

NAT-Based, Route-Path, One-Armed

Though not as common, it is possible to do NAT-based SLB with only one connection to the Layer 2 infrastructure, as shown in Figure C-8. There are two subnets; however, they all exist on the same LAN. This is topologically identical to the flat-based, route-path, one-armed scenario.

It is also not common to use DSR with a NAT-based topology. This requires a Layer 3 device with interfaces on the public and private networks, as does the load balancer, to forward the already processed packets to the Internet in order to take the outbound load off the load balancer. Figure C-9 shows this type of sce-

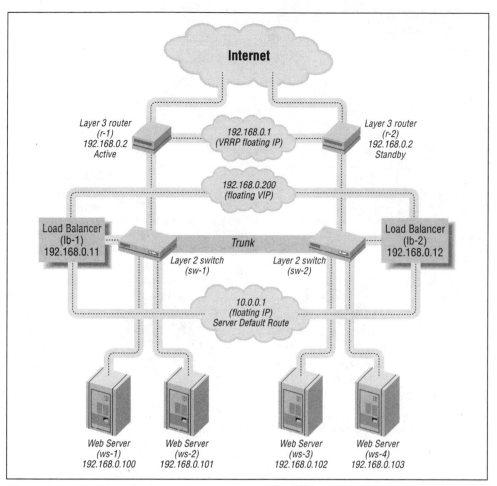

Figure C-8. A NAT-based, route-path, one-armed SLB implementation

nario with redundancy components removed to better show the concept (but redundancy is still very possible with this scenario).

It is also possible to implement NAT-based DSR with a one-armed configuration. The router just needs to be multinetted with both 192.168.0.1 and 10.0.0.1 (the server's default route) on the same interface. This configuration is shown in Figure C-10.

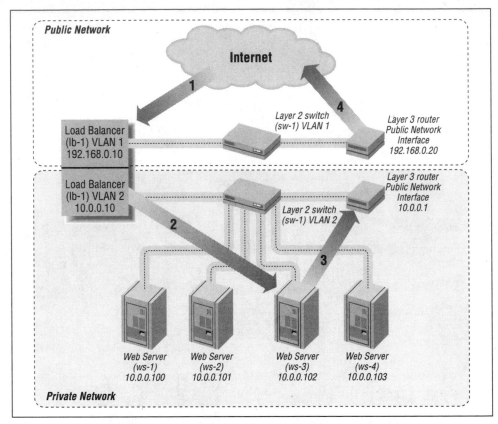

Figure C-9. A NAT-based, two-armed DSR implementation

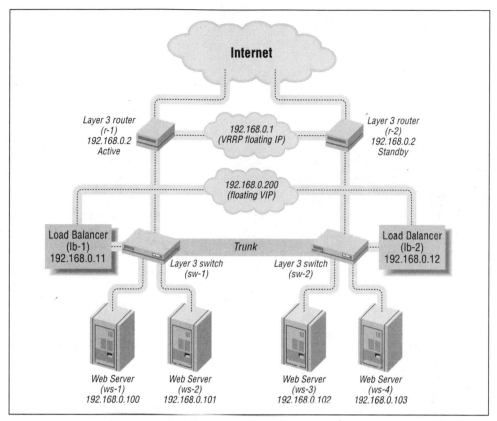

Figure C-10. A NAT-based, one-armed DSR implementation

Index

We'd like to hear your suggestions for improving our indexes. Send email to *index@oreilly.com.*

VIPs (Virtual Servers), Alteon, 88–90
  NAT-based SLB, 94–95
VMA (Virtual Matrix Architecture), 37
VPN (Virtual Private Network), NAT-based
      SLB and, 71
VR (Virtual Router), 95
VRID (Virtual Router ID), 95
VRRP (Virtual Router Redundancy
      Protocol), 19–20
  ESRP and, 20
  routers and, 47

W

the wall, 36–38
WANs (Wide Area Networks), GSLB
      and, 10
web servers, 52
  configuration, DSR, 154–155
  flat-based SLB and, 59
  NAT-based SLB and, 68
web site resources, xii

web sites, DNS entries, 5
Web stores, traffic patterns, 36
Web traffic ratio, 28
WebNS (Web Network Services)
  access levels, 103
  administration network, 117
  commands, 145–149
  content rules, 107
  CSS switches and, 100
  encryption and, 104
  owners
      flat-based SLB, 107
      NAT-based SLB, 111–113
WebOS (Alteon), commands, 141–142
whois utility, DNS servers and, 6
Windows 2000 loopback interface
      configuration, DSR, 153–154
WUI (Web User Interface)
  administration, 120–124
  see also CLI (Command Line Interface)

About the Author

Tony Bourke is a private consultant specializing in Unix administration, networking, and load balancing. He has held positions at SiteSmith, GlobalCenter, and Digex. Tony has designed and implemented SLB and Unix architectures for many high-profile and high-traffic web sites. He has published articles in *Sys Admin Magazine*, *Hostingtech Magazine*, and *Network World*. He is one of the leading authorities on the topic of Server Load Balancing and frequently speaks at conferences around the country. He can be reached at *tony@vegan.net*.

Colophon

Our look is the result of reader comments, our own experimentation, and feedback from distribution channels. Distinctive covers complement our distinctive approach to technical topics, breathing personality and life into potentially dry subjects.

The animal on the cover of *Server Load Balancing* is a jacana, a tropical wading bird. There are eight species of jacana, in six genera. The jacana's most remarkable physical characteristic is its long toes. In fact, the jacana has the longest toes (relatively speaking) of any living bird. When in flight, the jacana's toes extend beyond the tip of the its tail. These long, wide-spread toes enable the jacana to walk across the floating leaves of water plants, hence, the names "lotus bird" and "lily trotter," by which some species of jacana are known. As useful as they are when walking on watery surfaces, the jacana's toes make walking on land very difficult, and for this reason you will rarely see a jacana walking on solid ground. For that matter, you will probably never see a jacana at all, as very few of them are found in captivity. They can be found in fresh-water ponds and swamps in tropical regions throughout the world. Jacanas feed mainly on insects, small mollusks, and small fish.

Jacana females are frequently larger than the males and are more aggressive. In most jacana species, the female mates with more than one male and lays more than one clutch of eggs per season. There are typically four glossy, "scribbled" eggs per clutch, laid in nests that float on the water. The male incubates the eggs and raises the young alone. Jacana chicks can swim and dive immediately after hatching. The father doesn't feed the young, as they are able to find and digest their own food, but he does protect and comfort them for the first few months of life.

Matt Hutchinson was the production editor and copyeditor for *Server Load Balancing*. Linley Dolby proofread the book. Nicole Arigo and Linley Dolby provided quality control. Johnna VanHoose Dinse wrote the index.

Emma Colby designed the cover of this book, based on a series design by Edie Freedman. The cover image is a 19th-century engraving from the Dover Pictorial Archive. Emma Colby produced the cover layout with QuarkXPress 4.1 using Adobe's ITC Garamond font.

David Futato designed the interior layout based on a series design by Nancy Priest. Neil Walls converted the files from Microsoft Word to FrameMaker 5.5.6 using tools created by Mike Sierra. The text and heading fonts are ITC Garamond Light and Garamond Book; the code font is Constant Willison. The illustrations that appear in the book were produced by Robert Romano and Jessamyn Read using Macromedia FreeHand 9 and Adobe Photoshop 6. This colophon was written by Clairemarie Fisher O'Leary.

Whenever possible, our books use a durable and flexible lay-flat binding. If the page count exceeds this binding's limit, perfect binding is used.